This book belongs to:

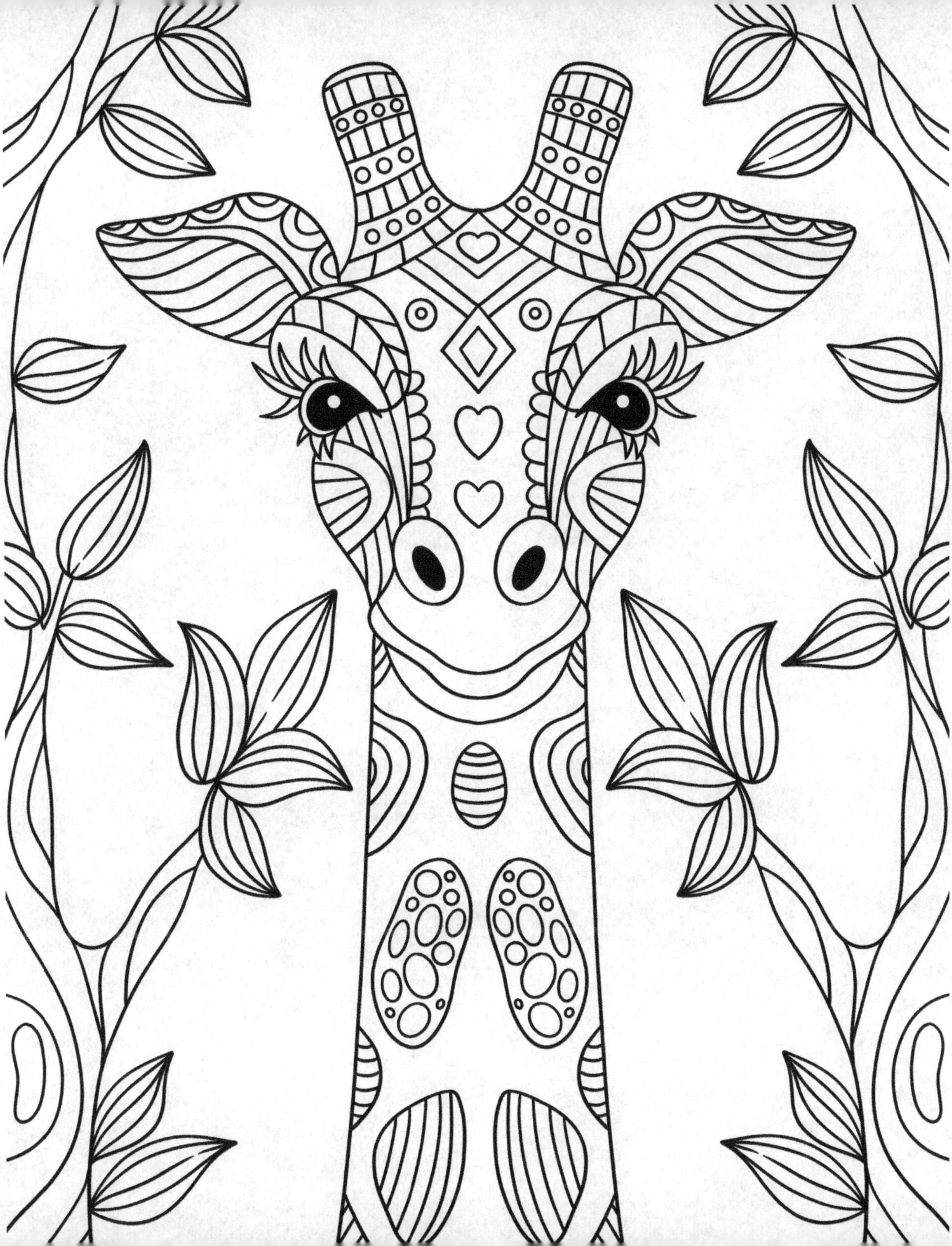

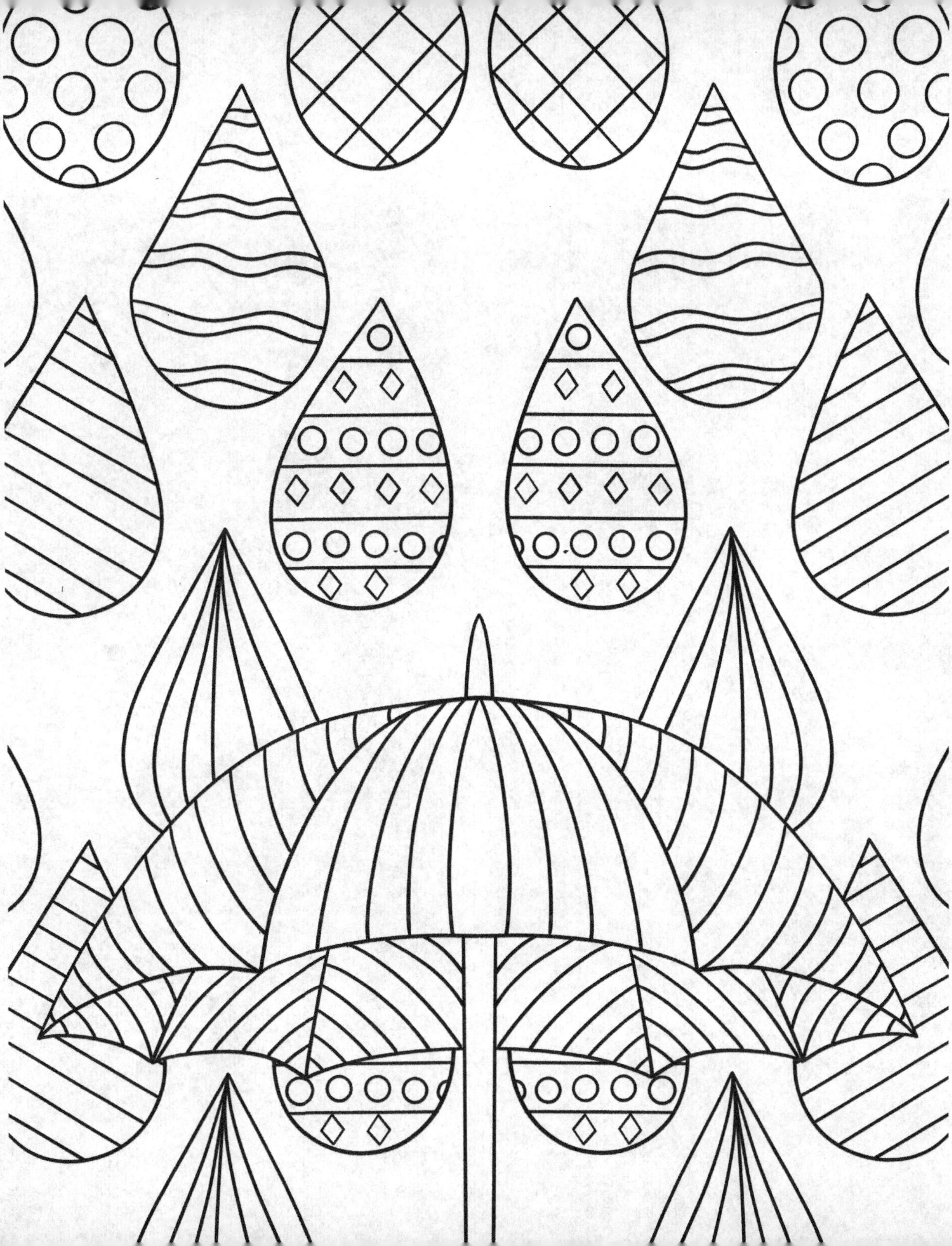

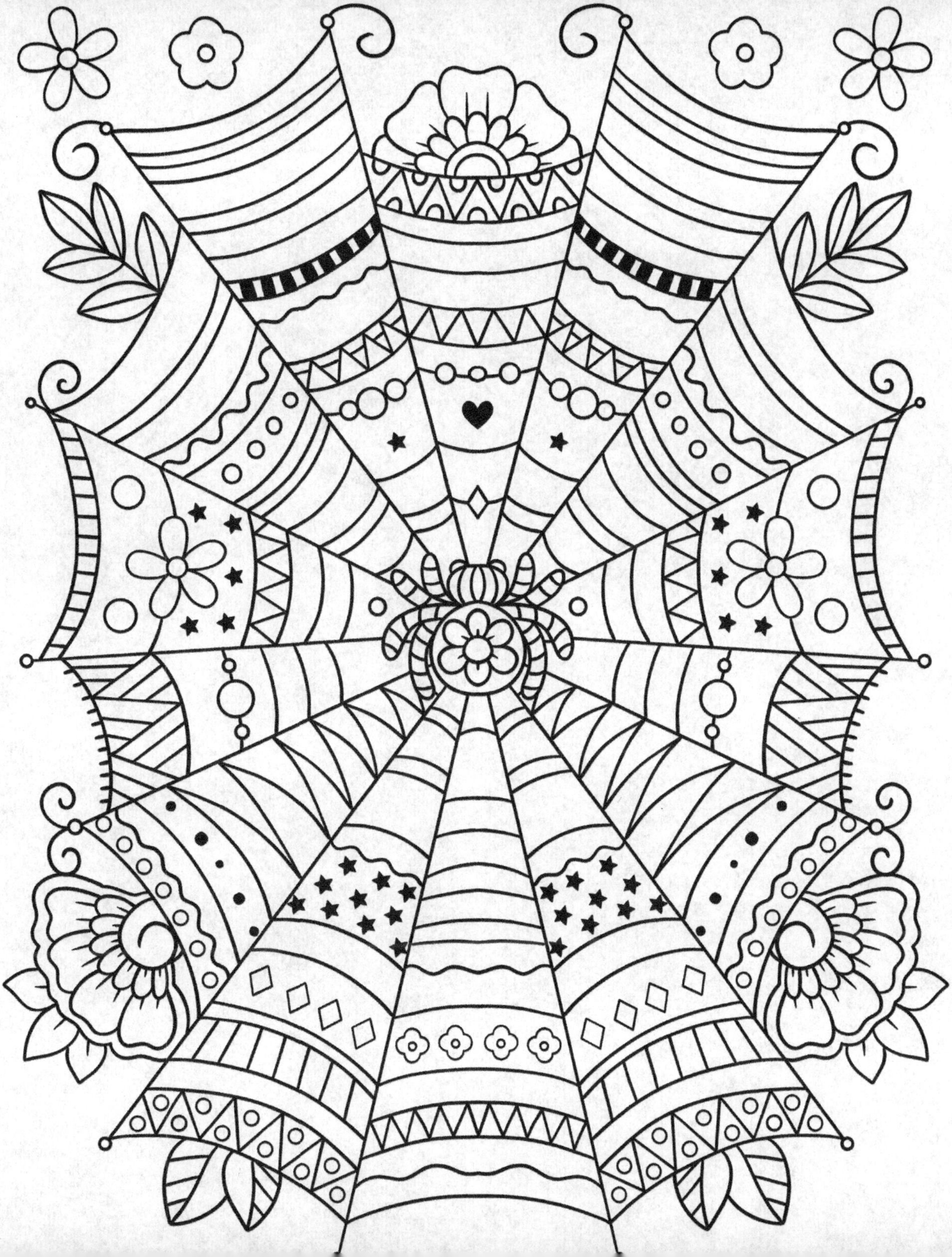

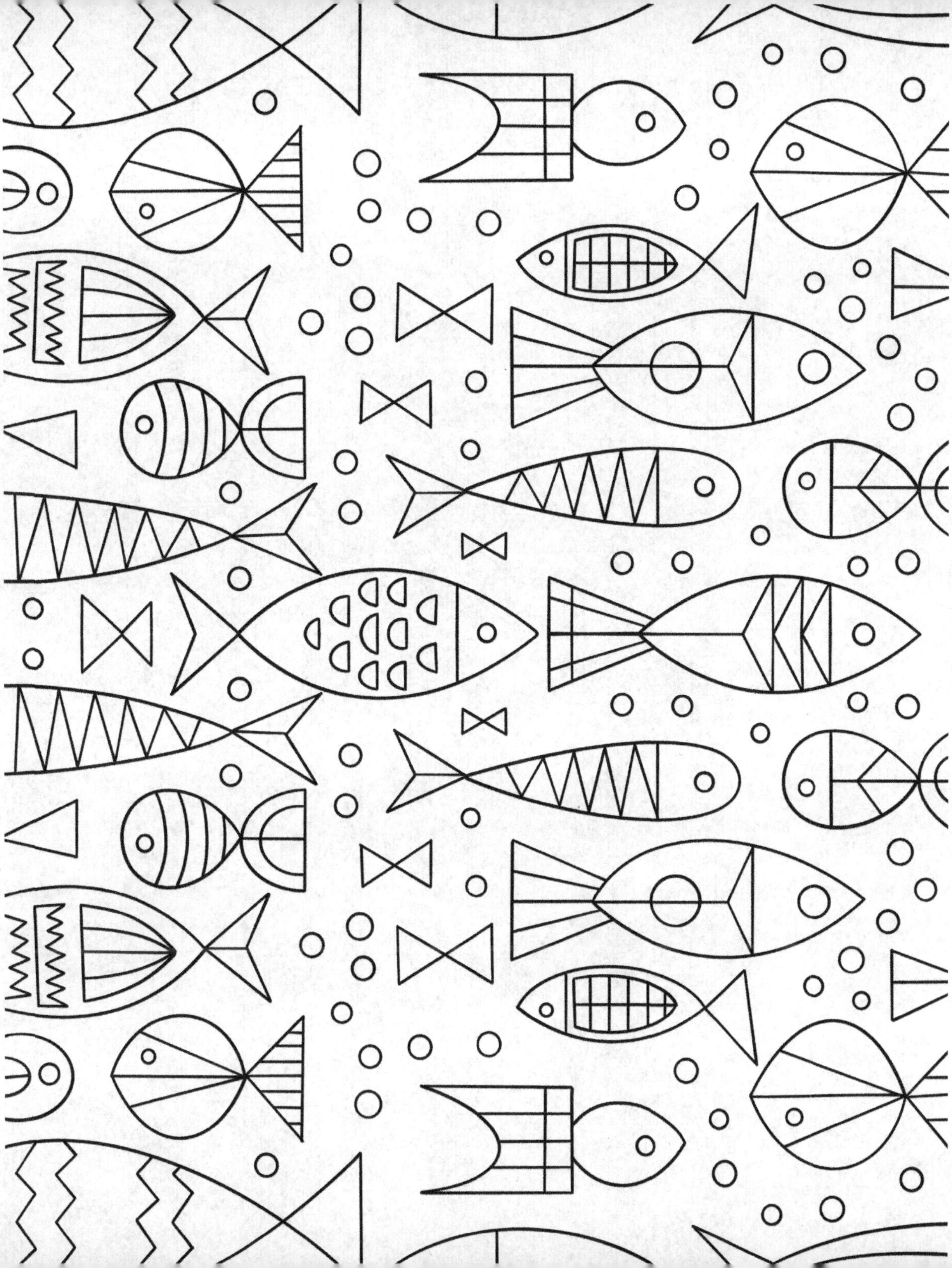

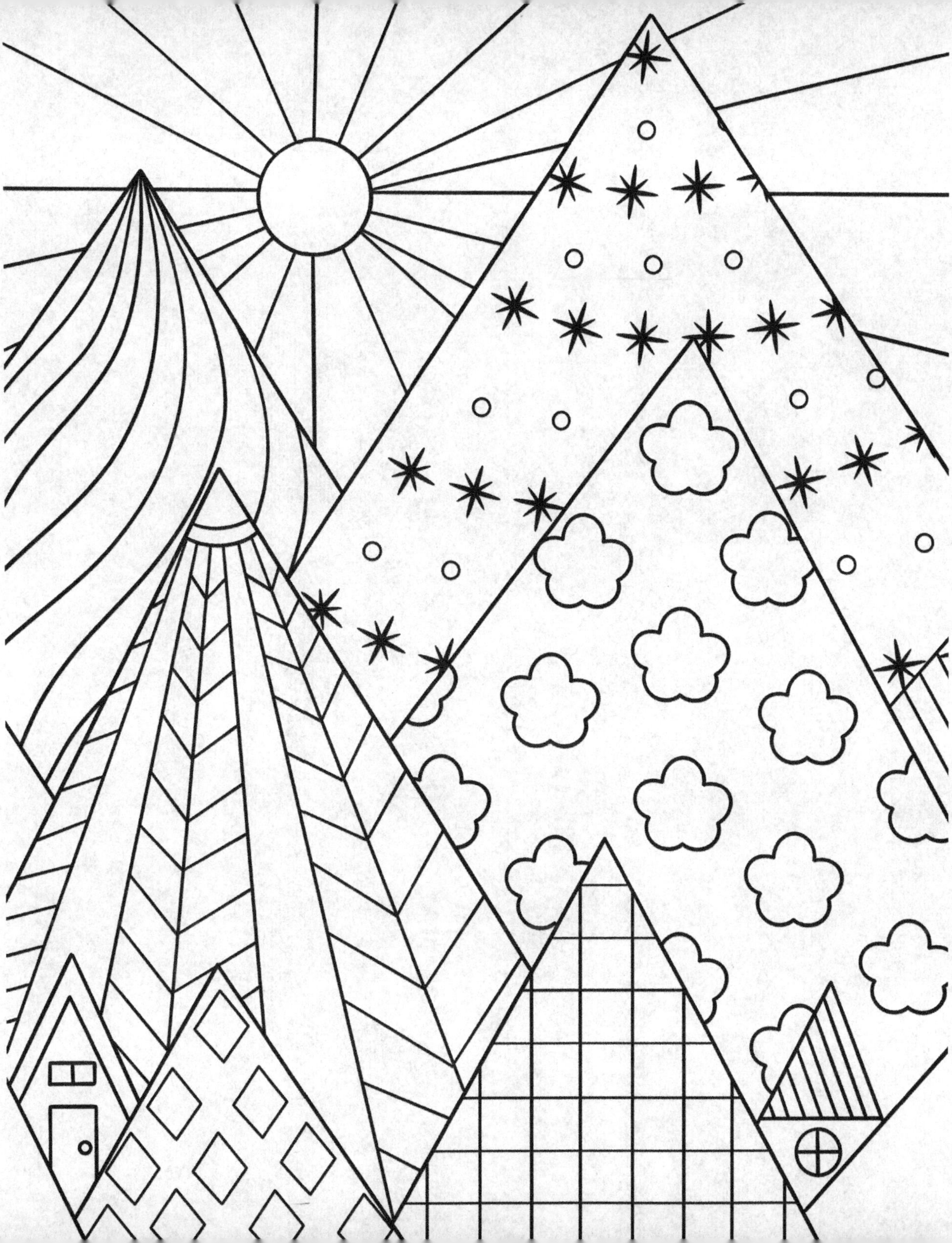

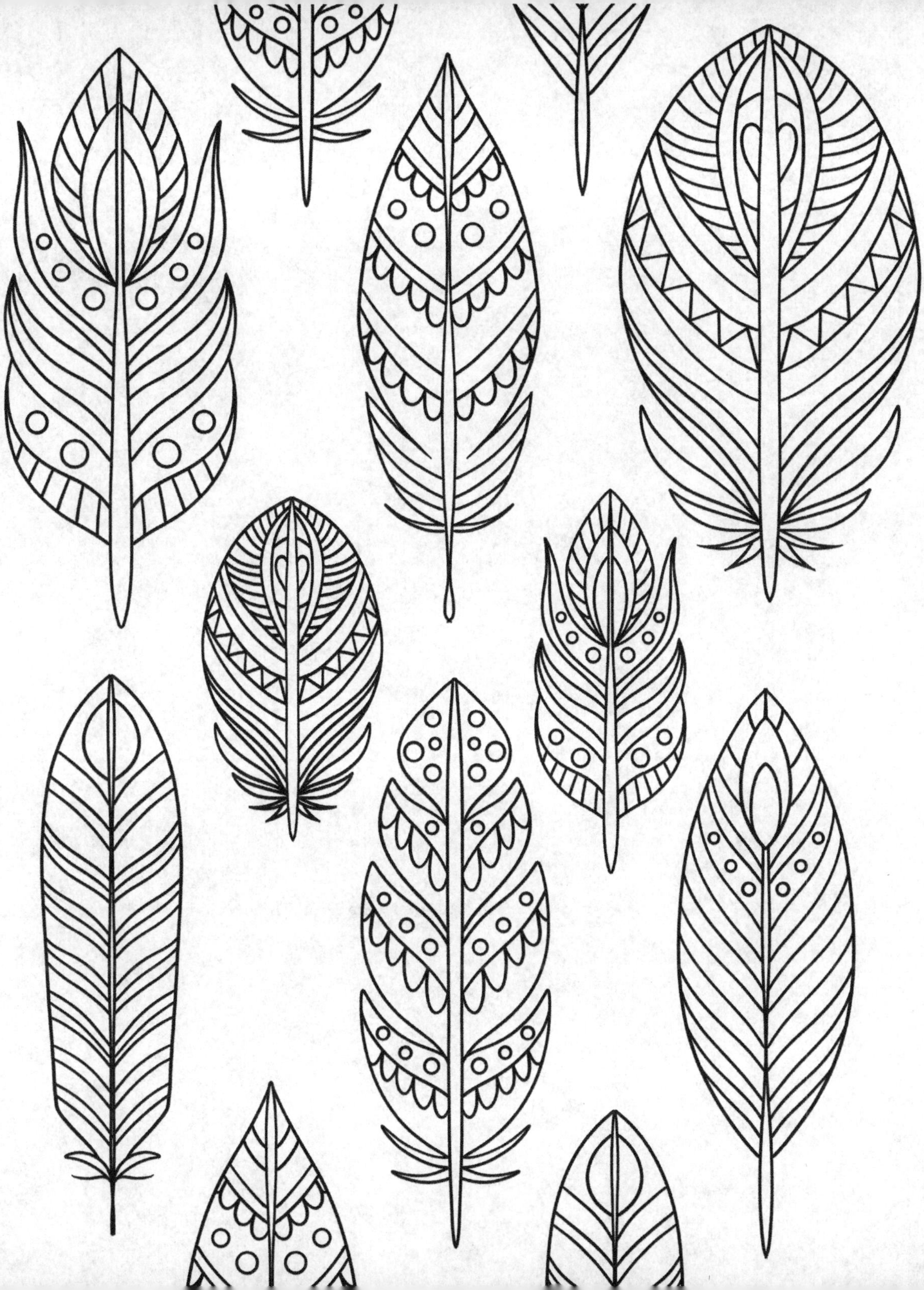

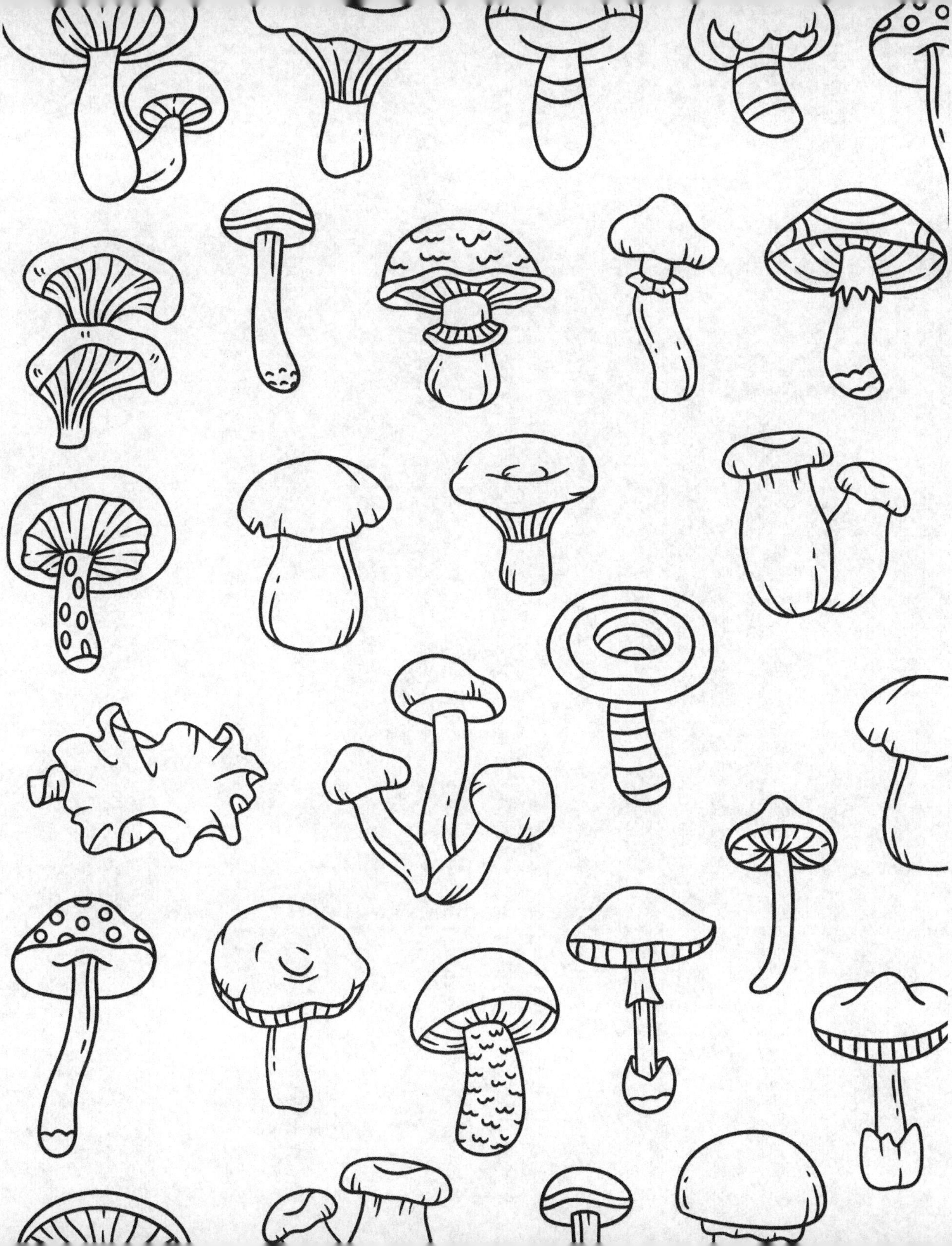

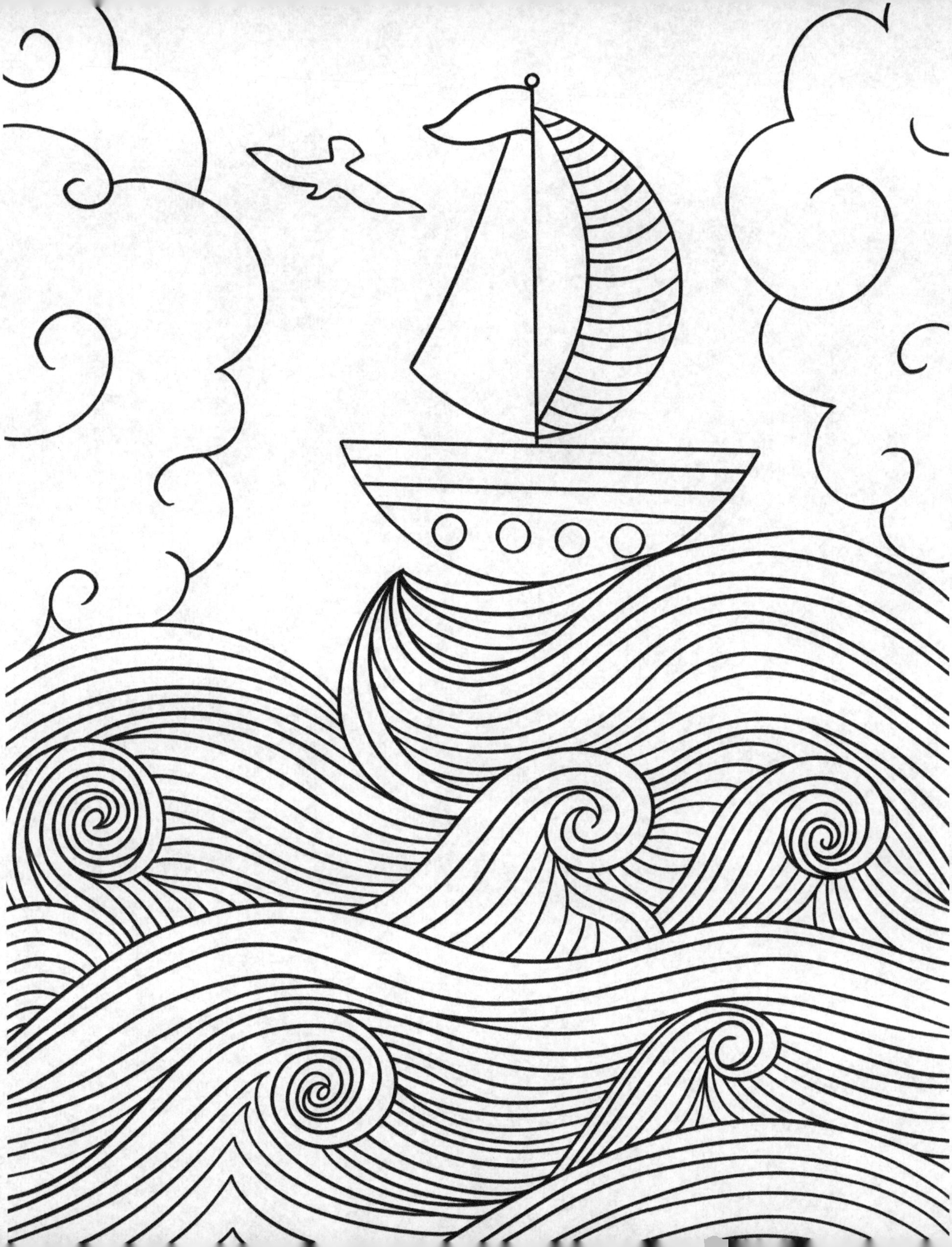

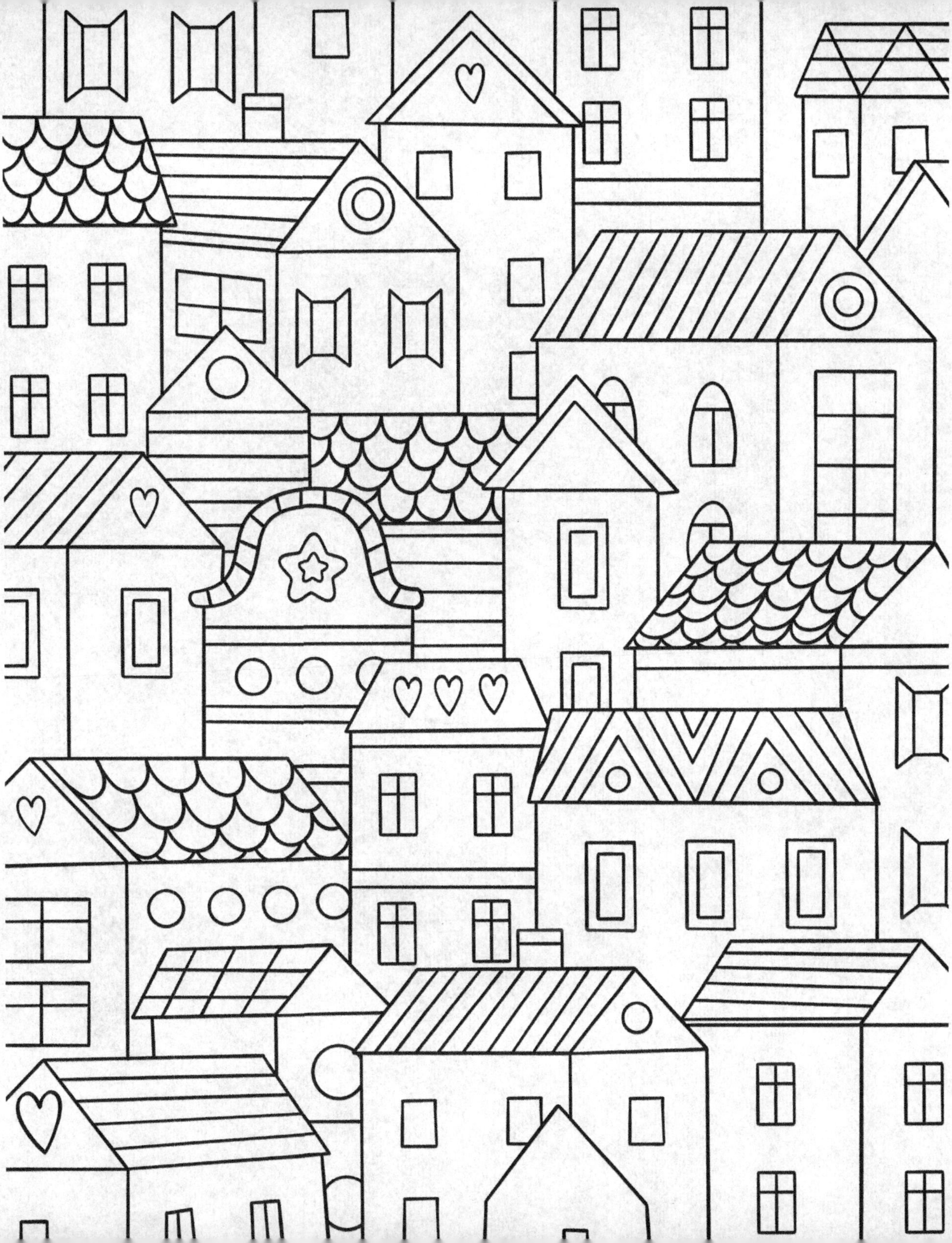

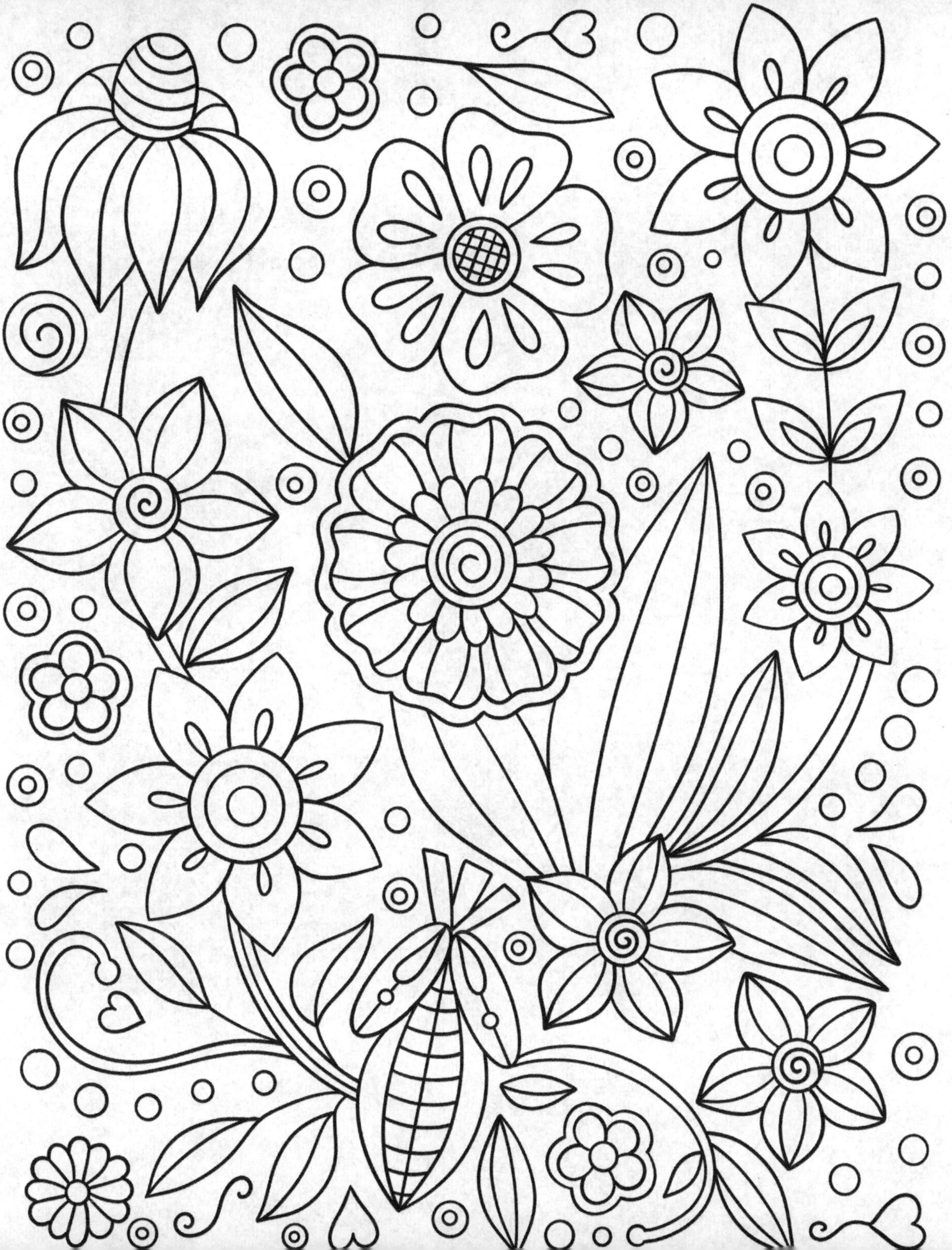

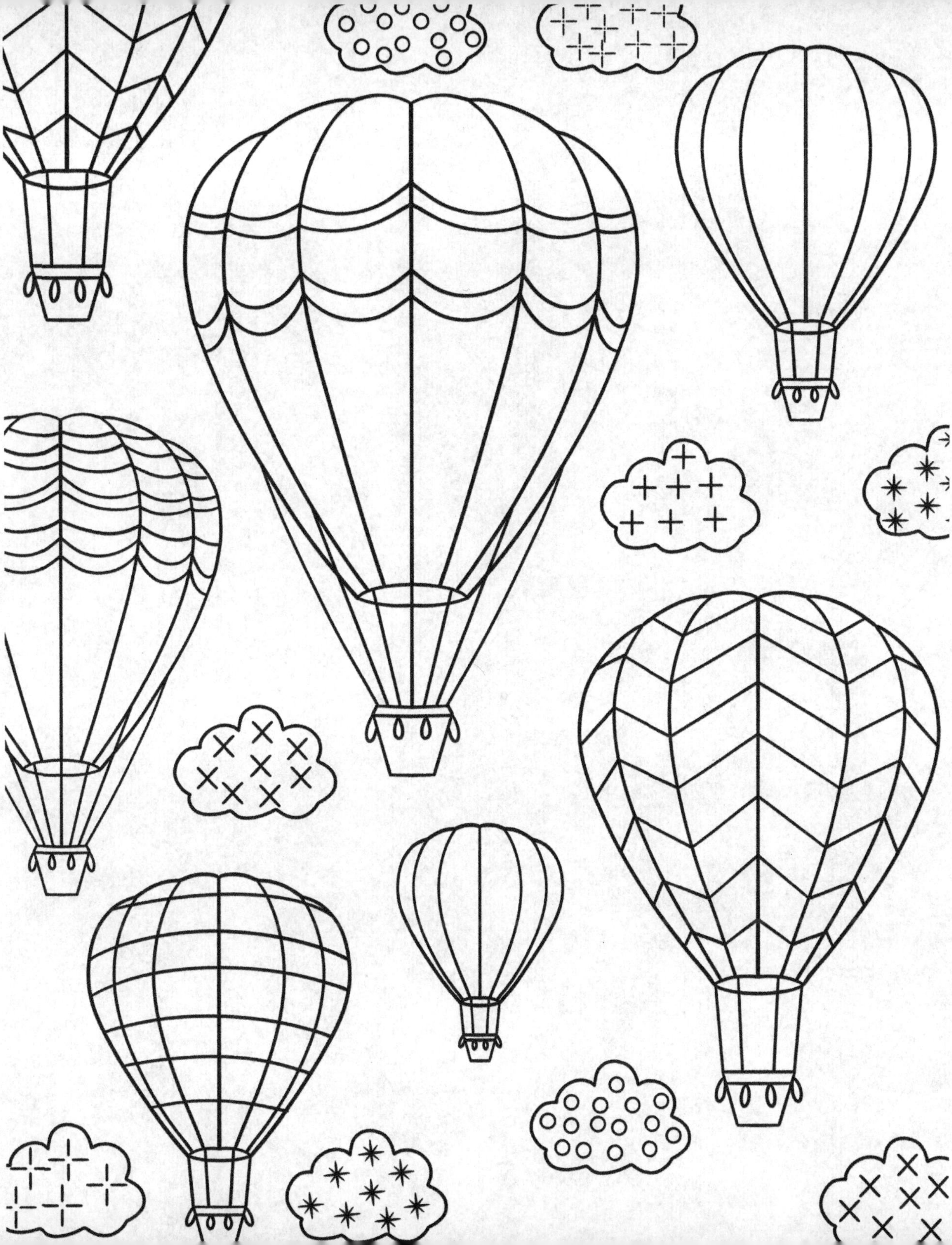

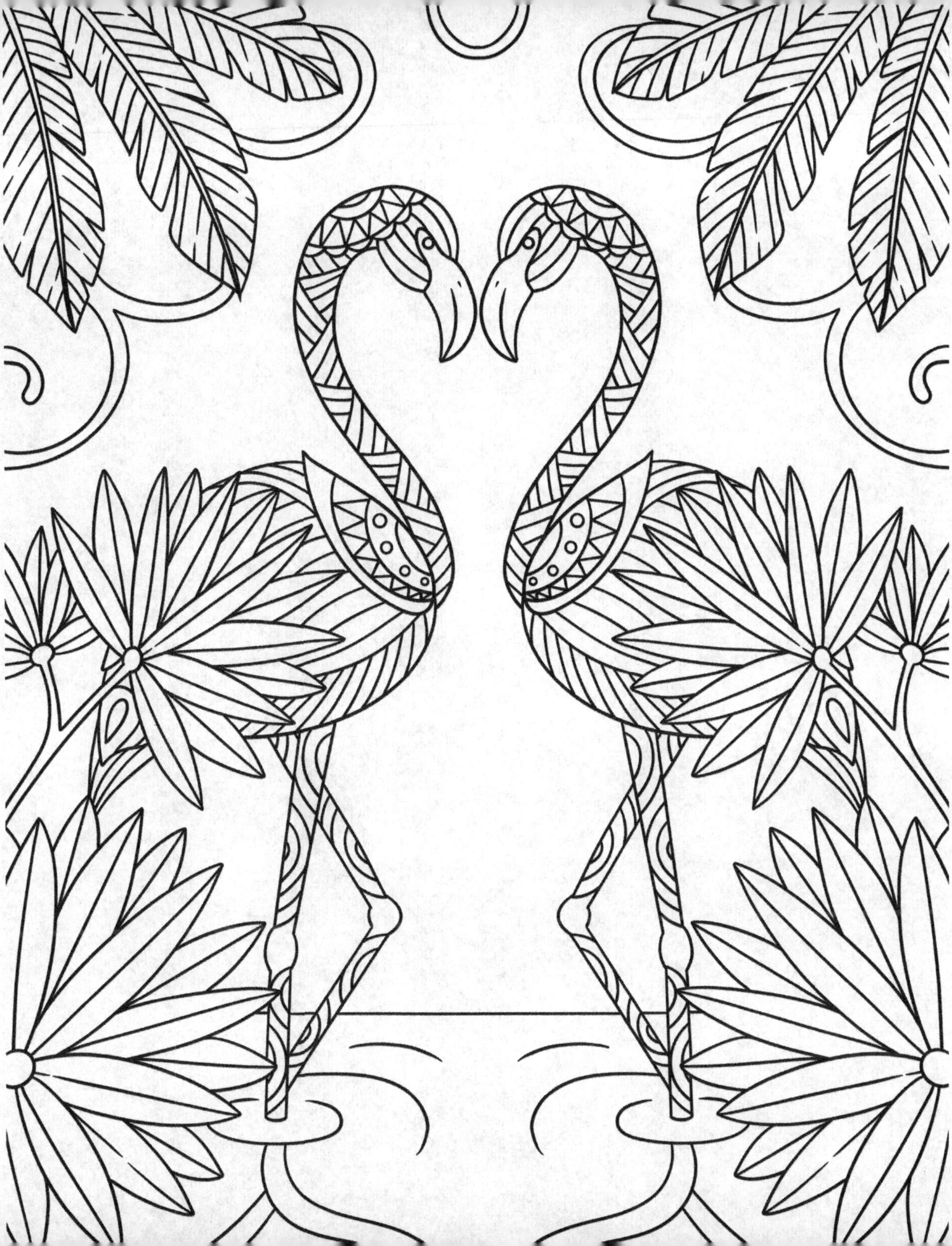

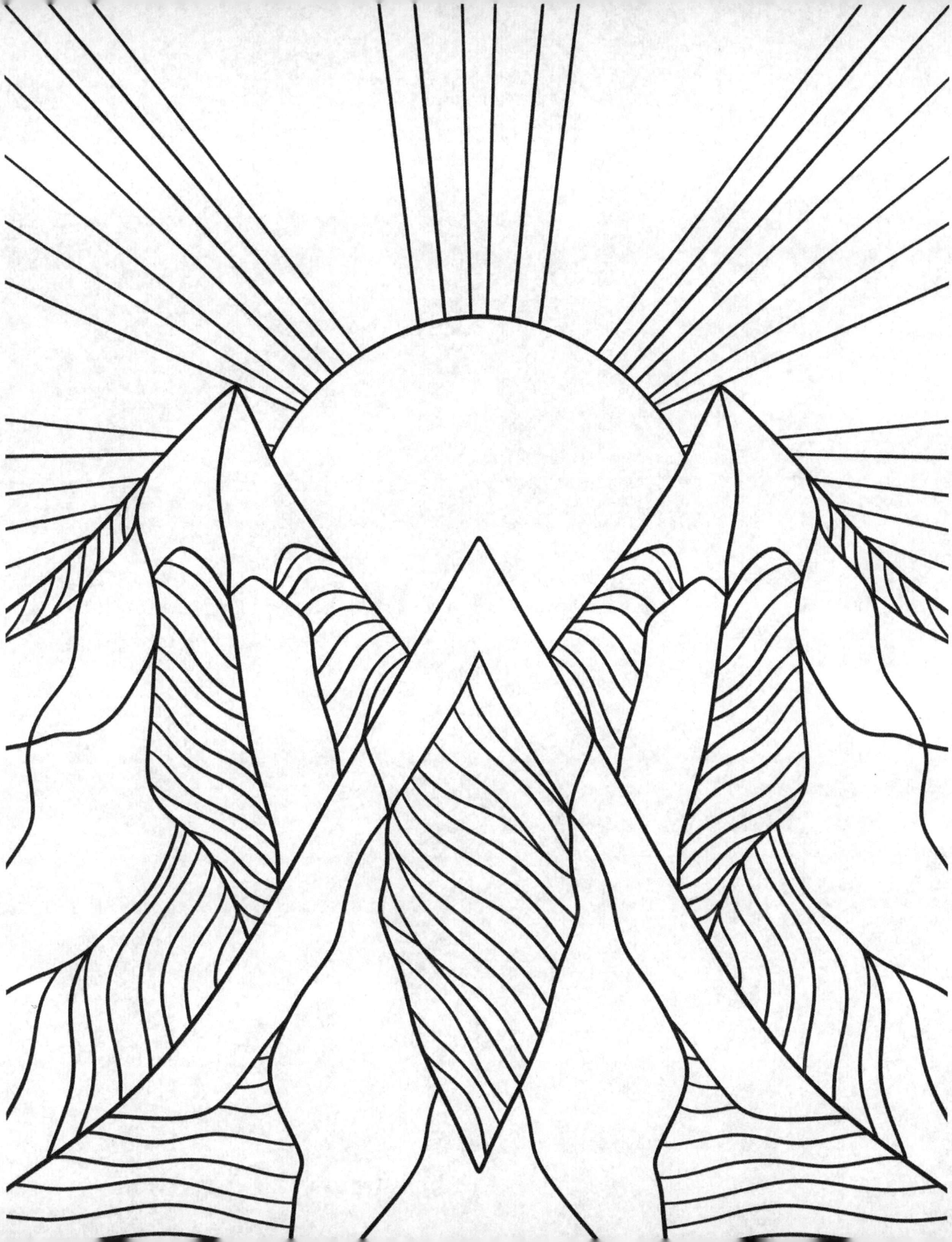

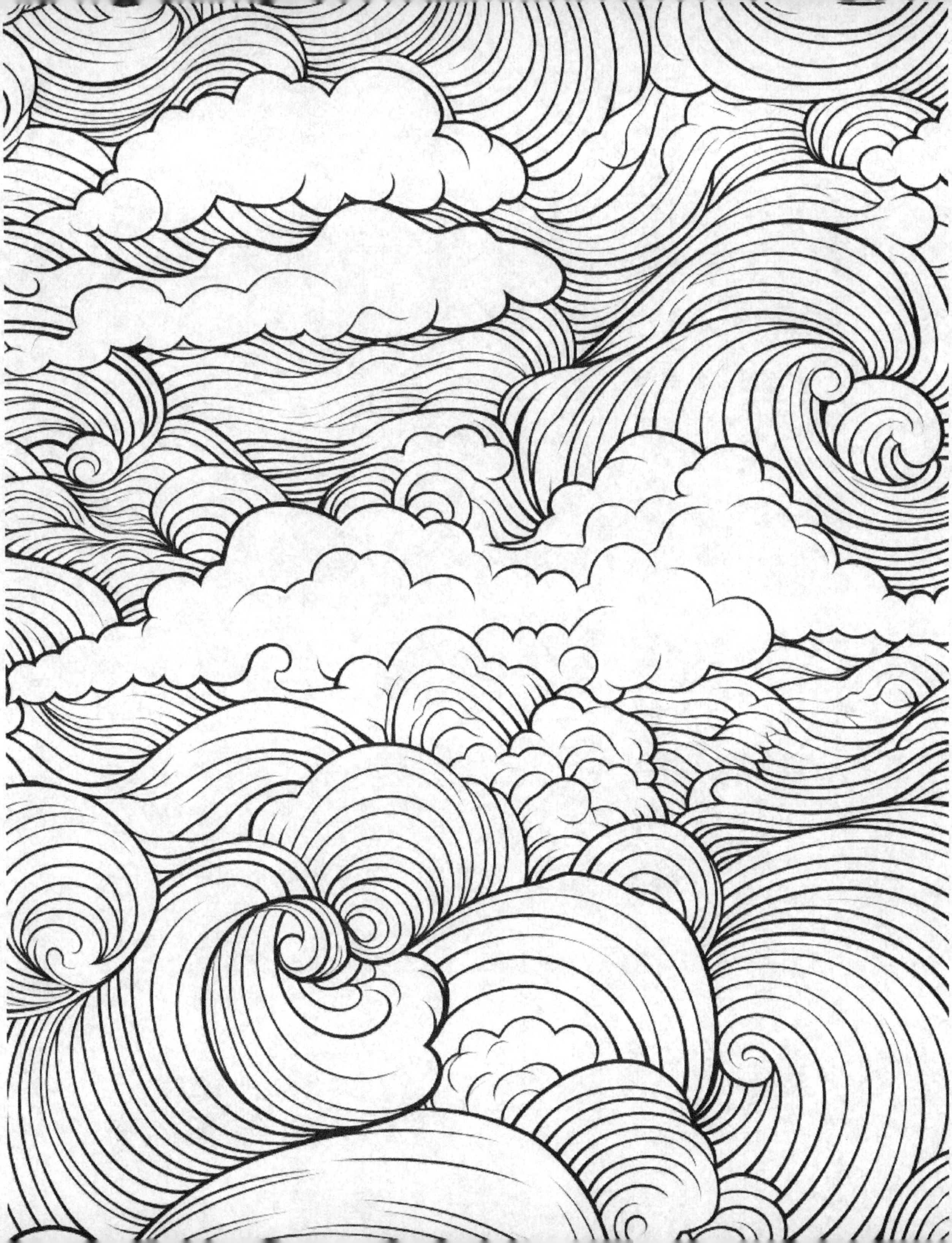

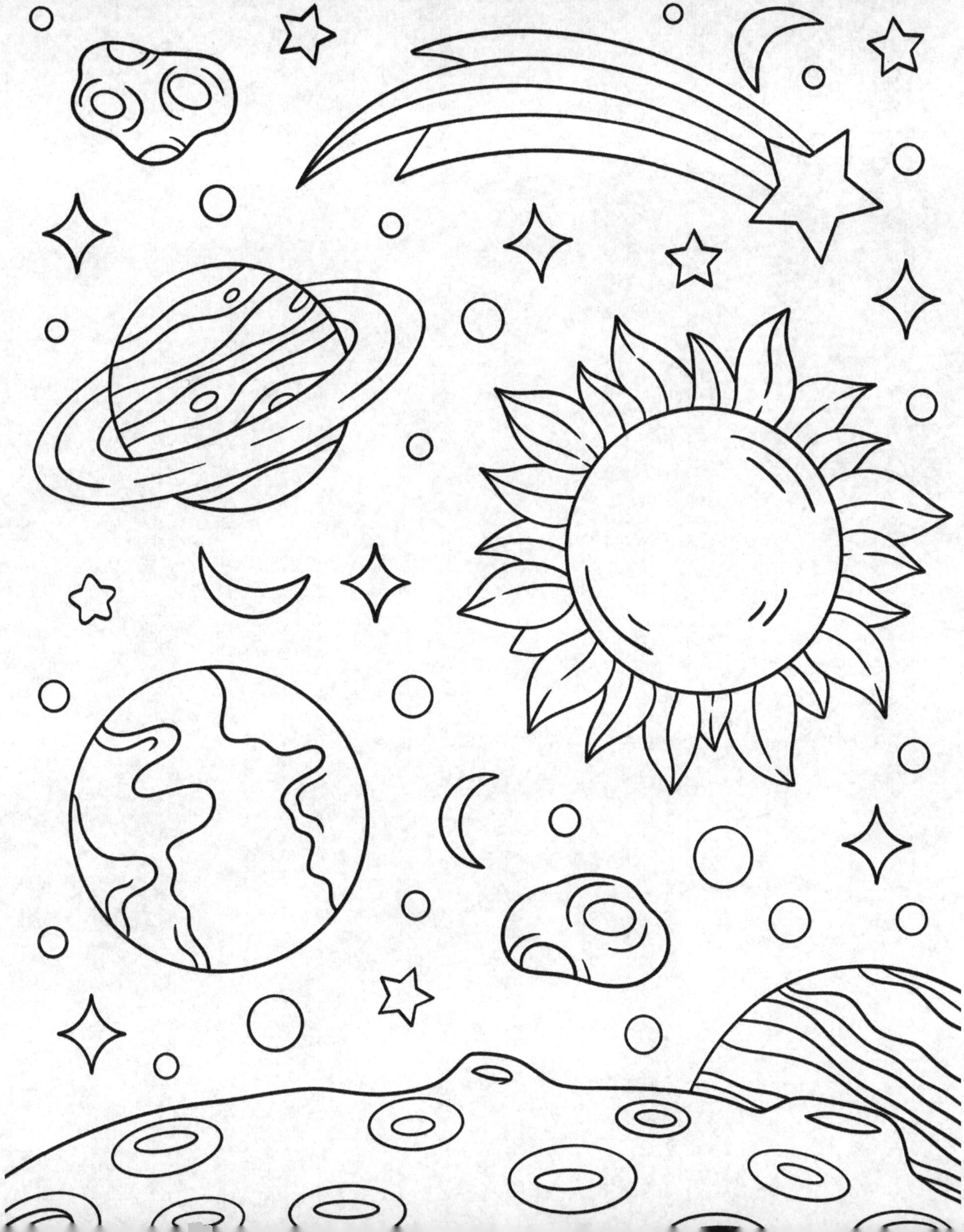

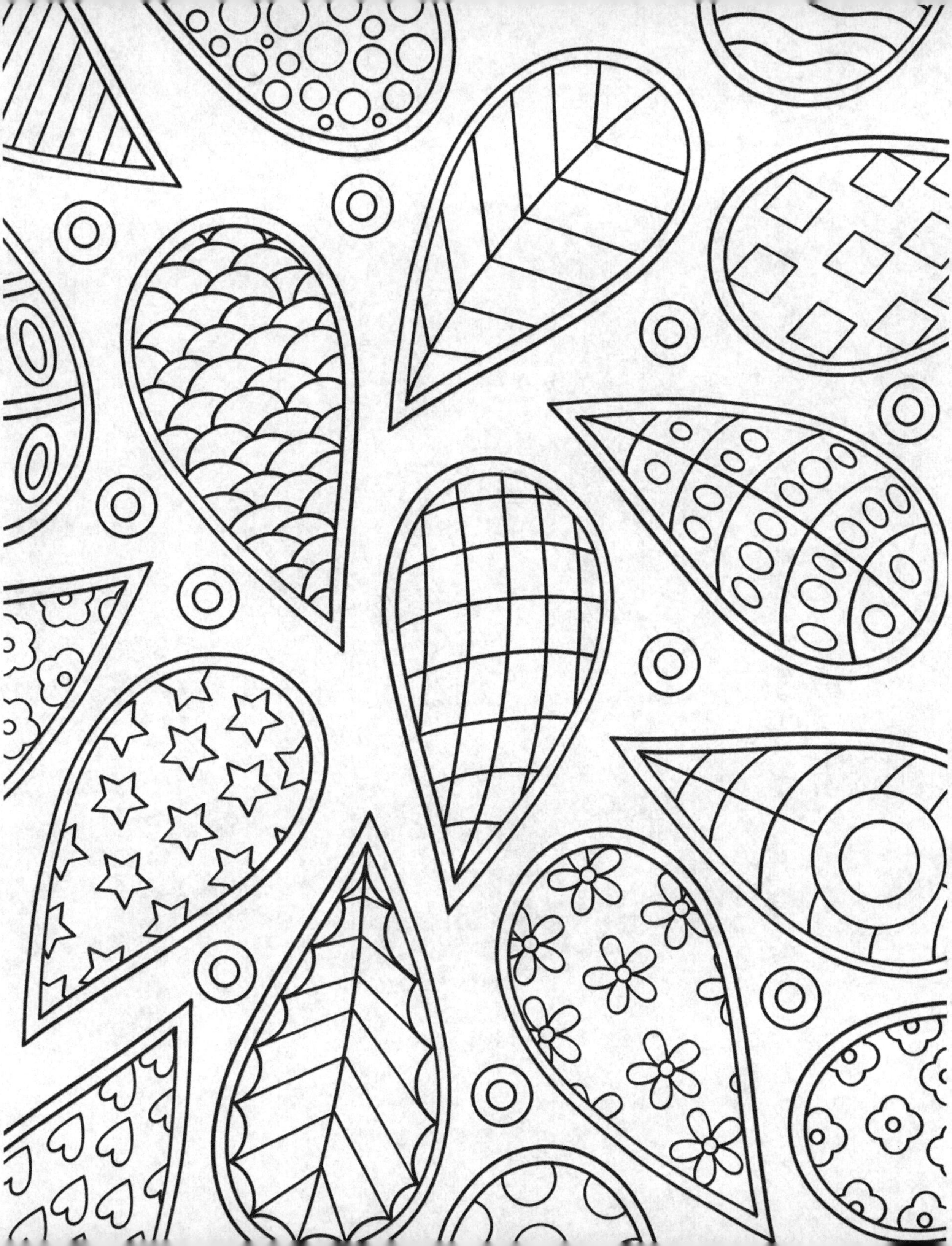

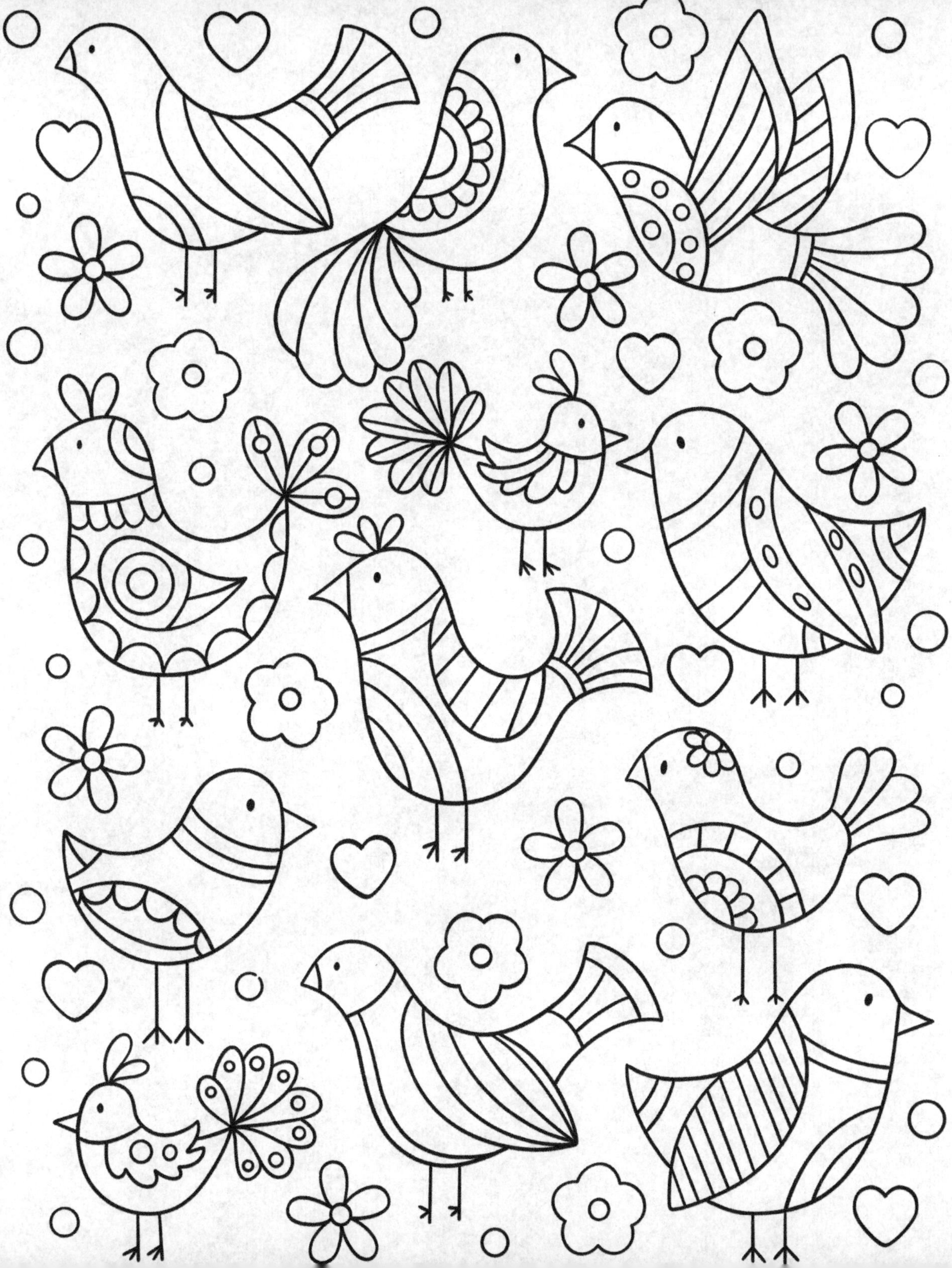

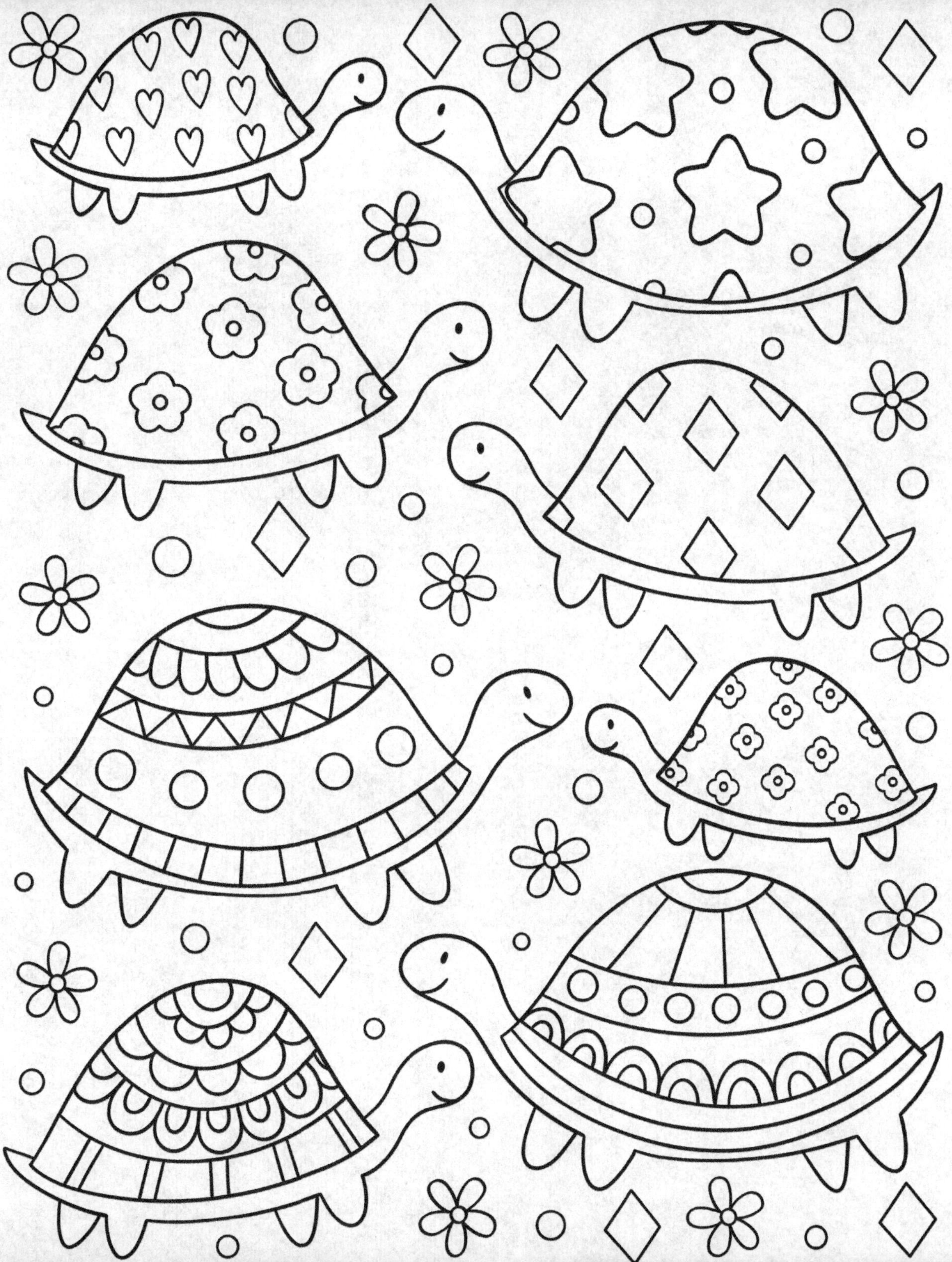

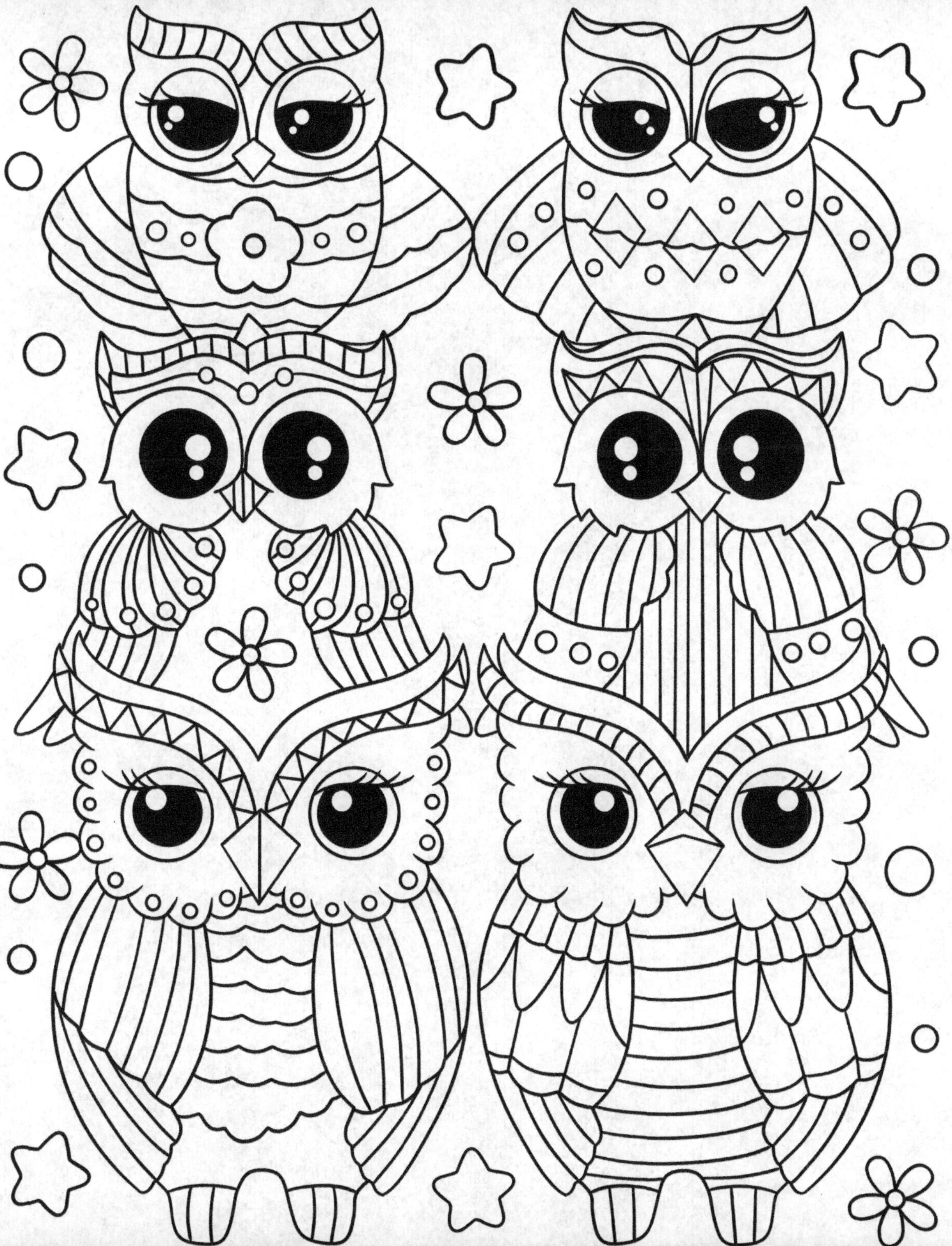

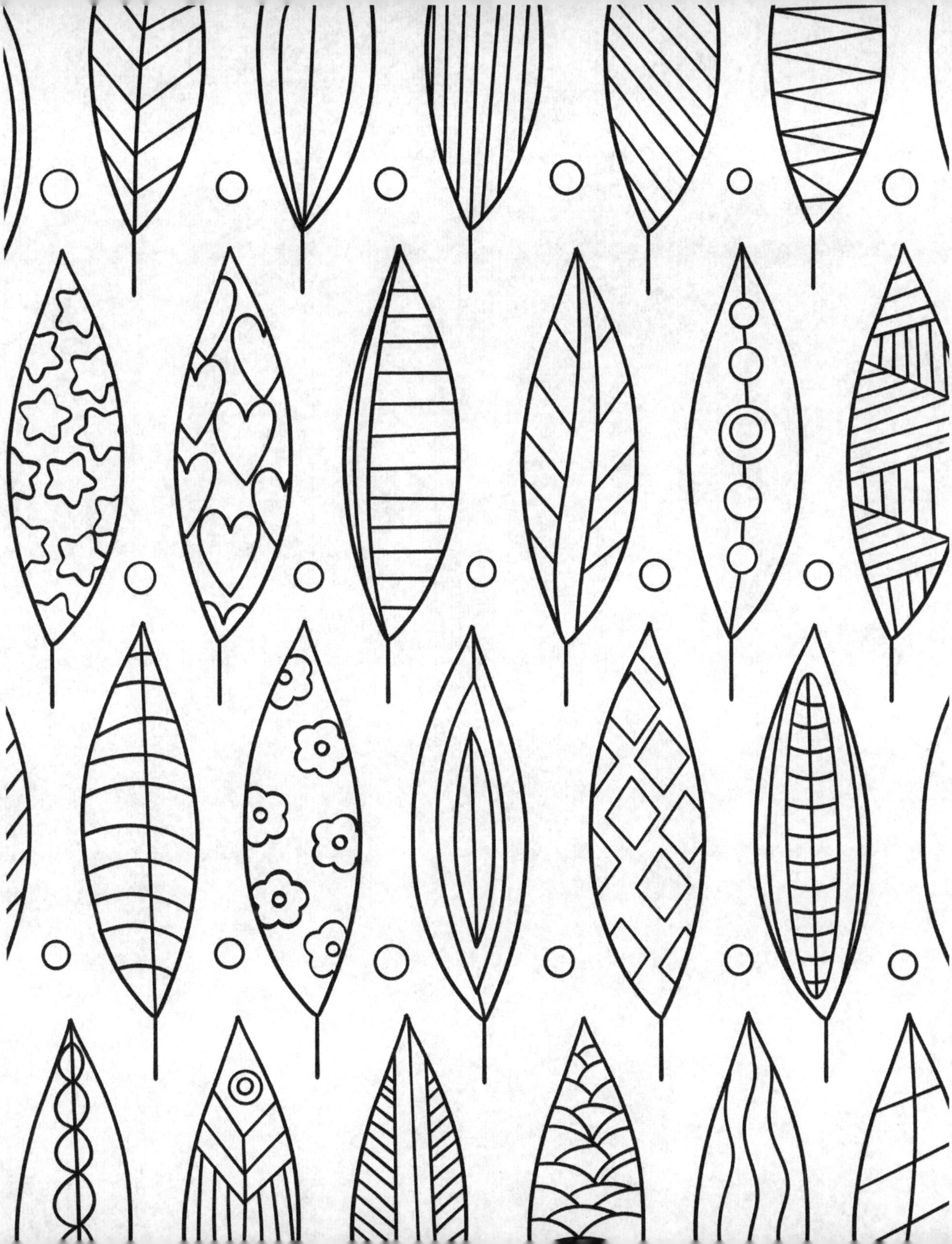

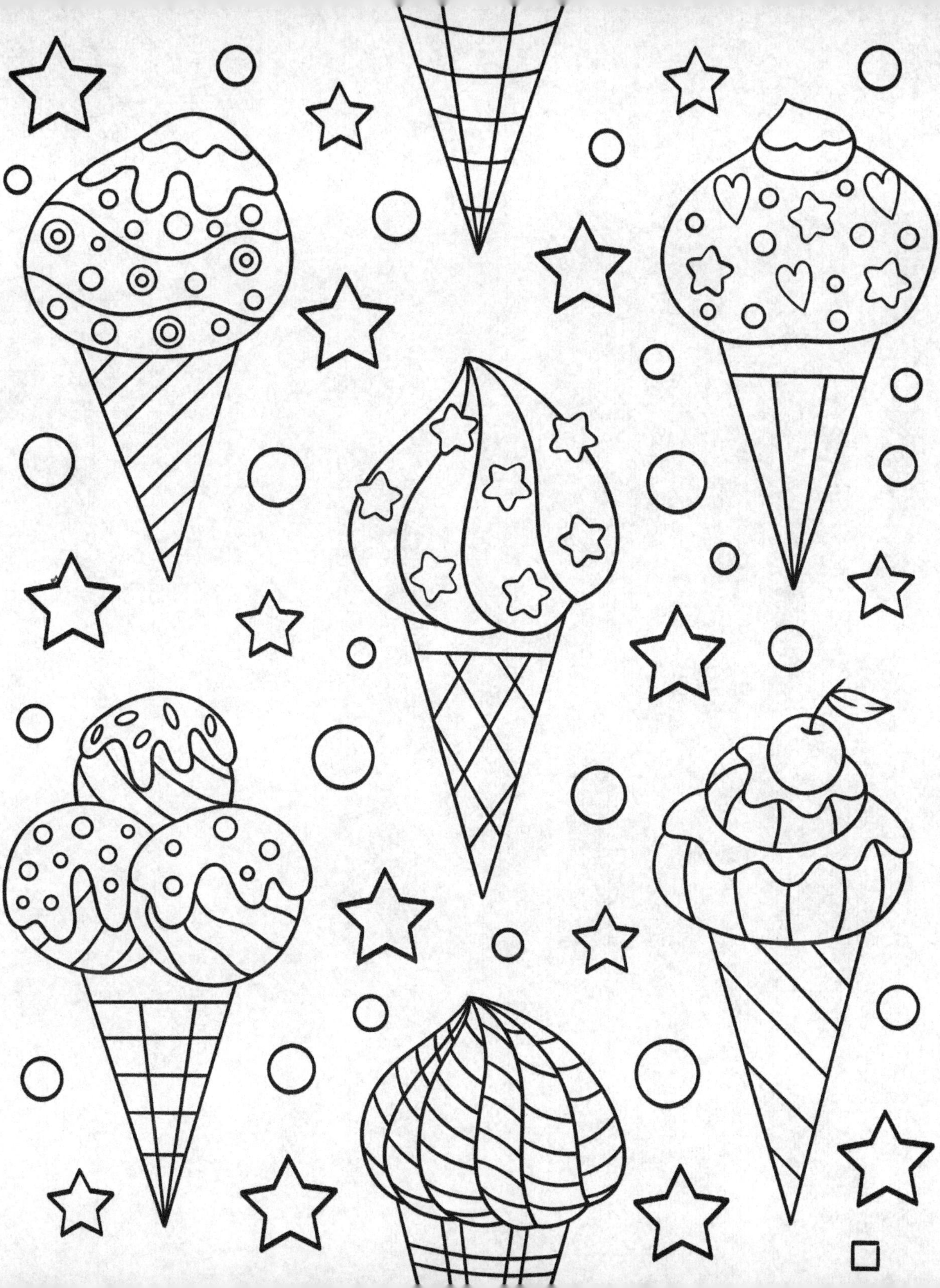

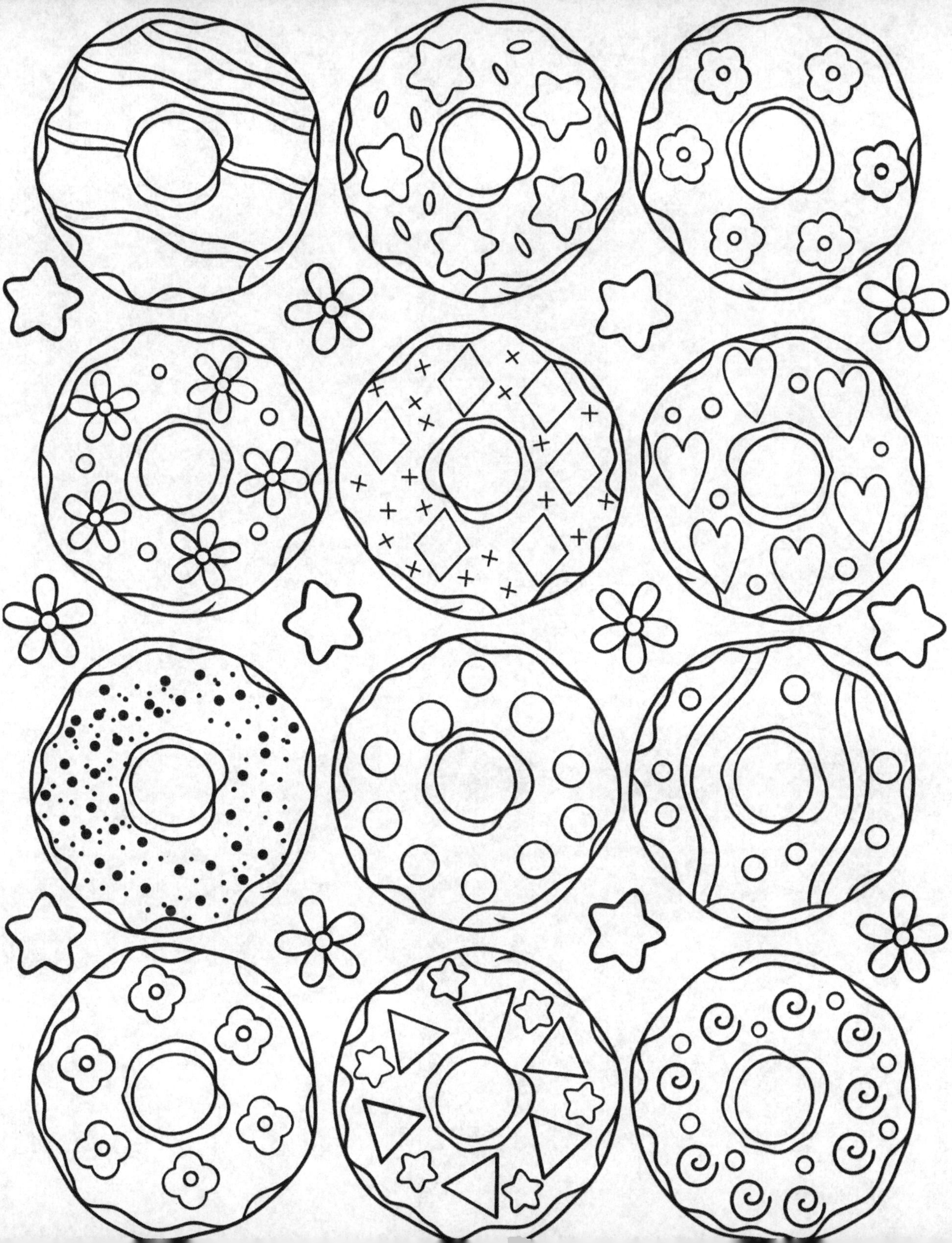

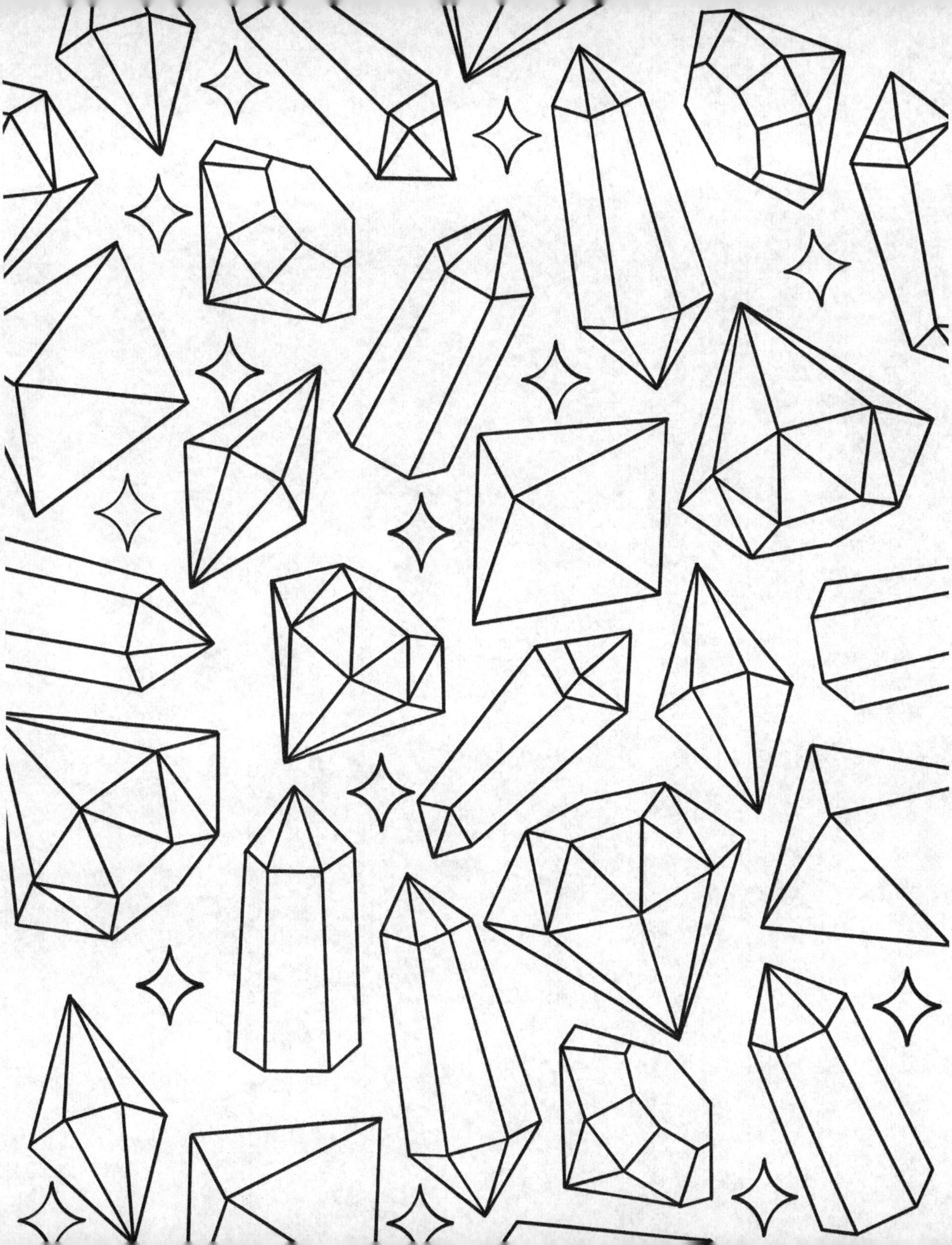

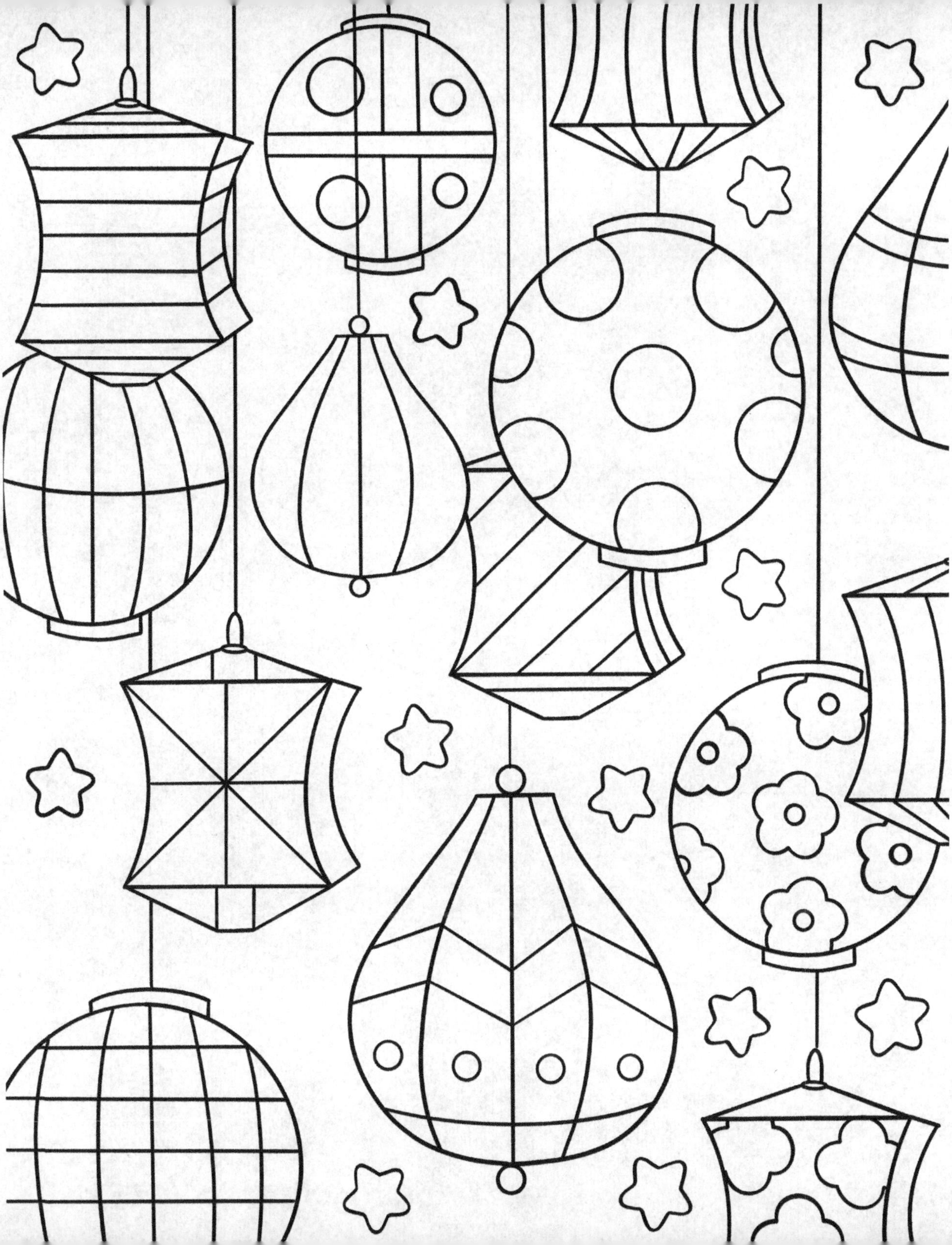

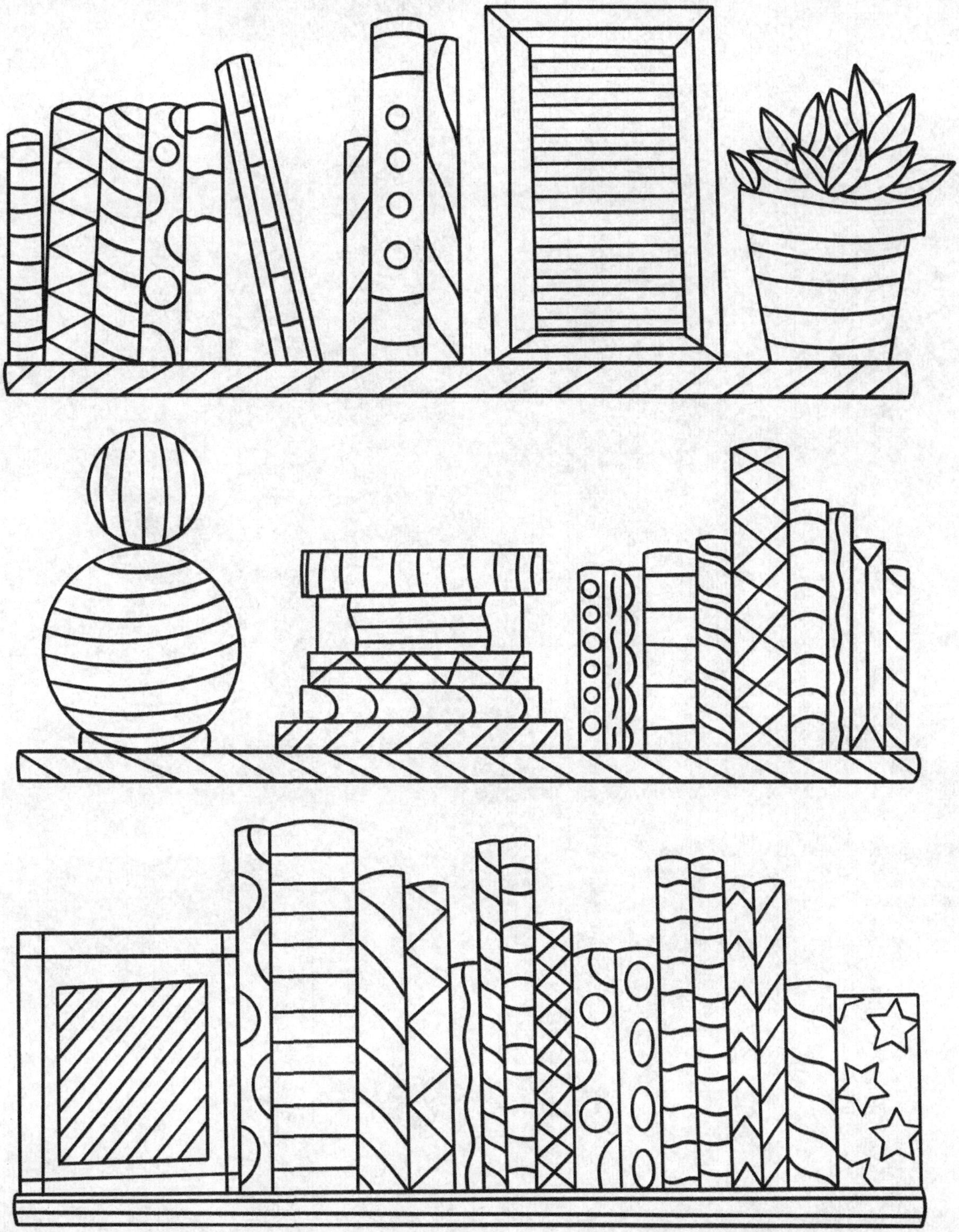

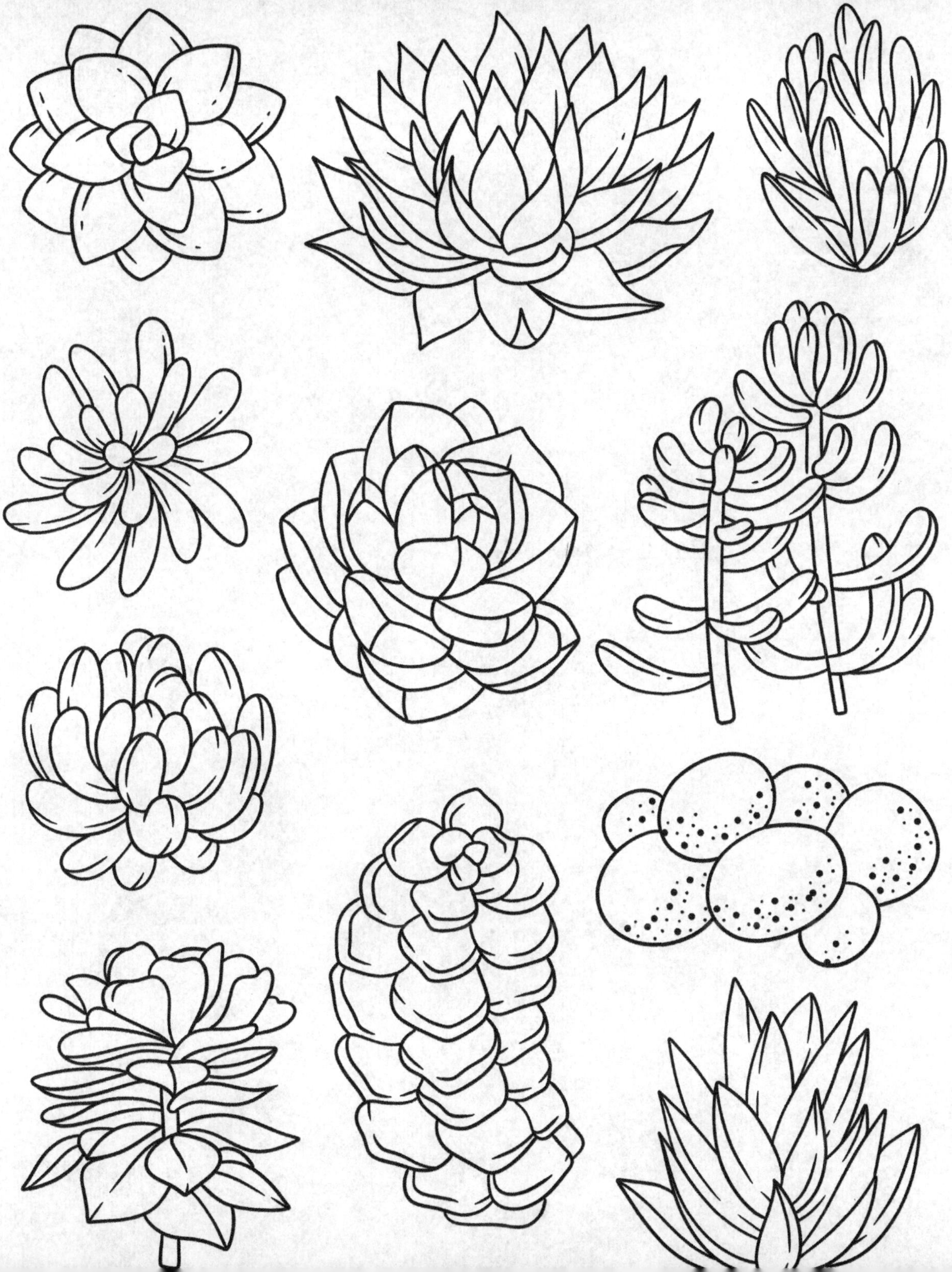

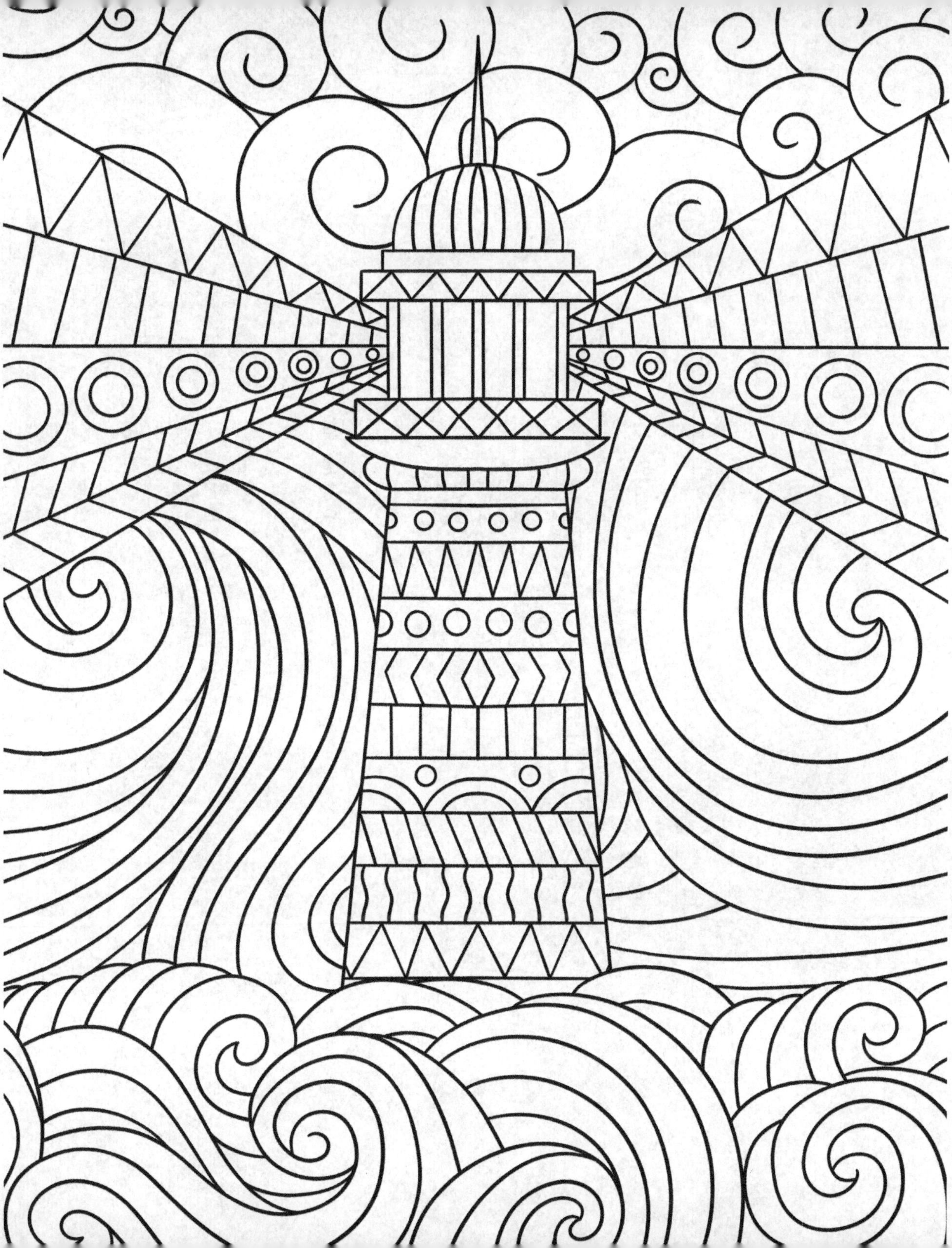

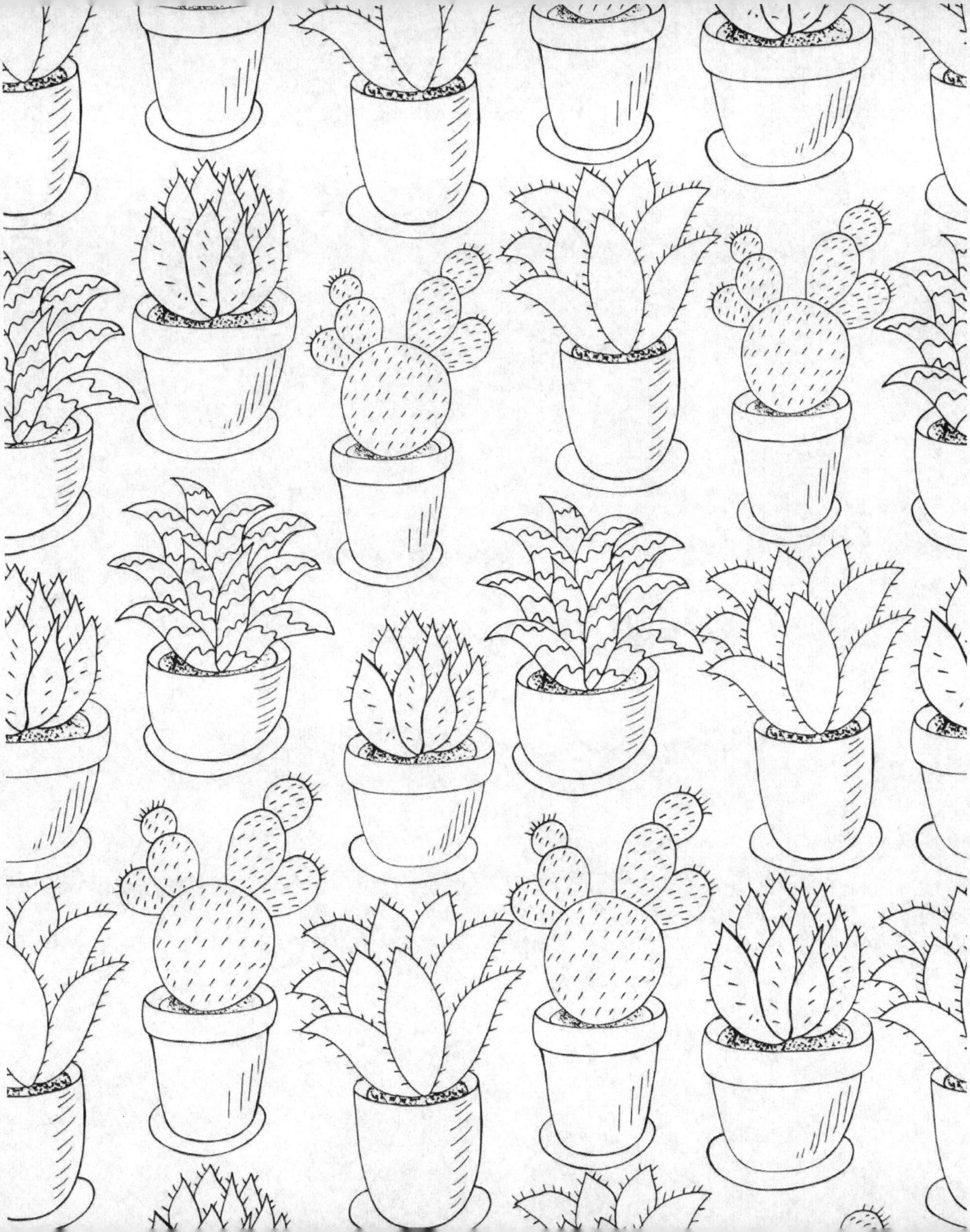

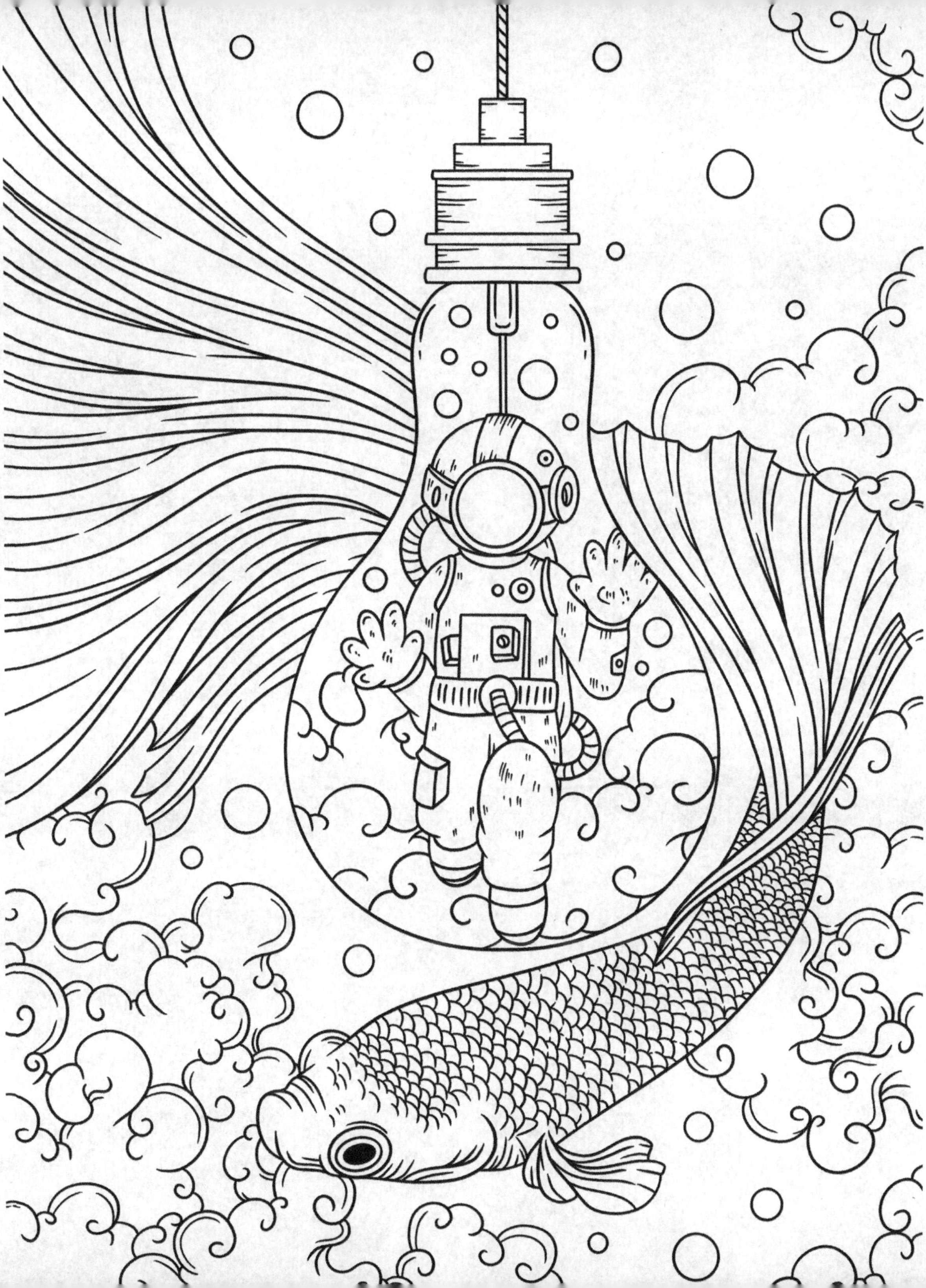

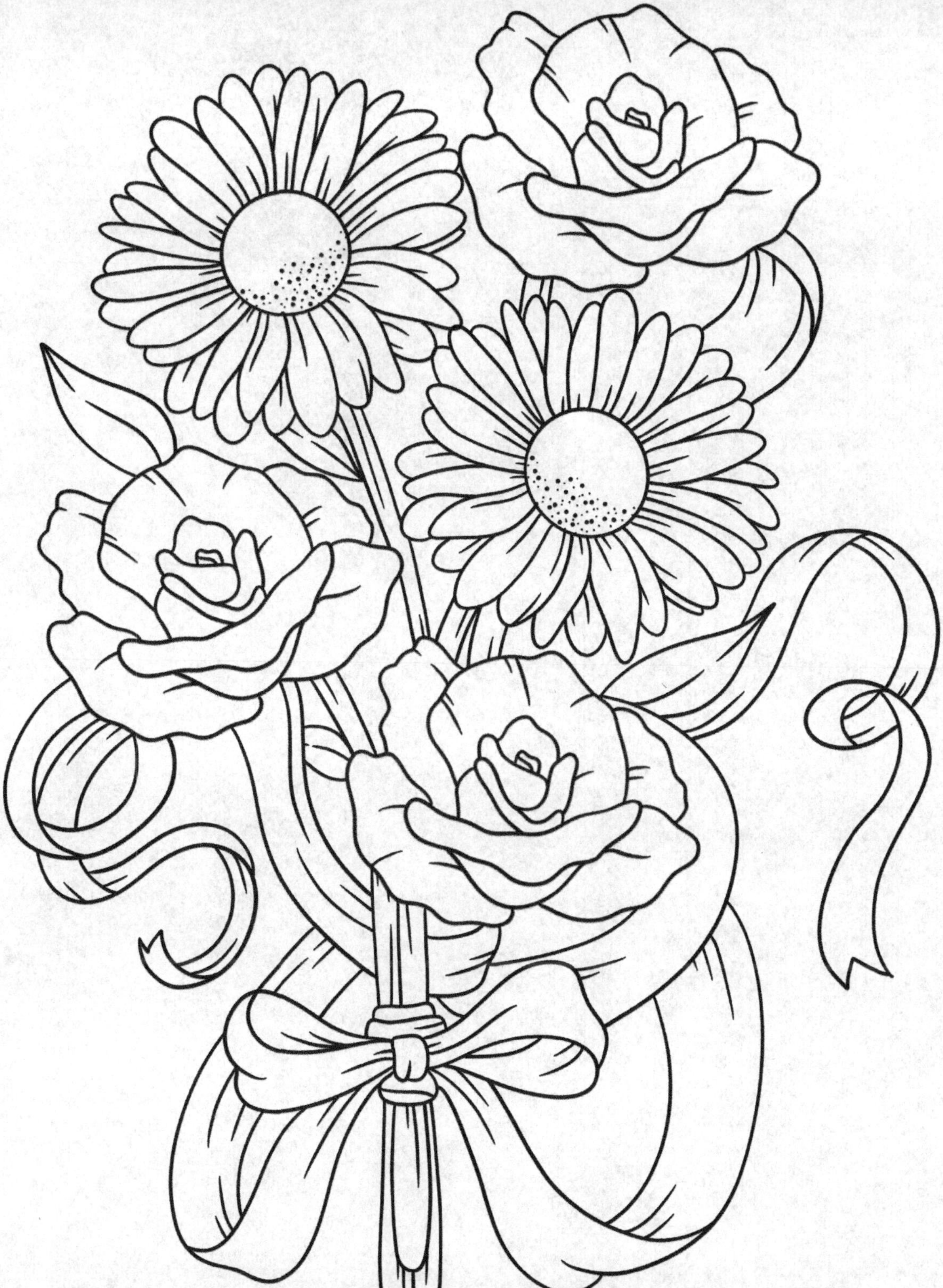

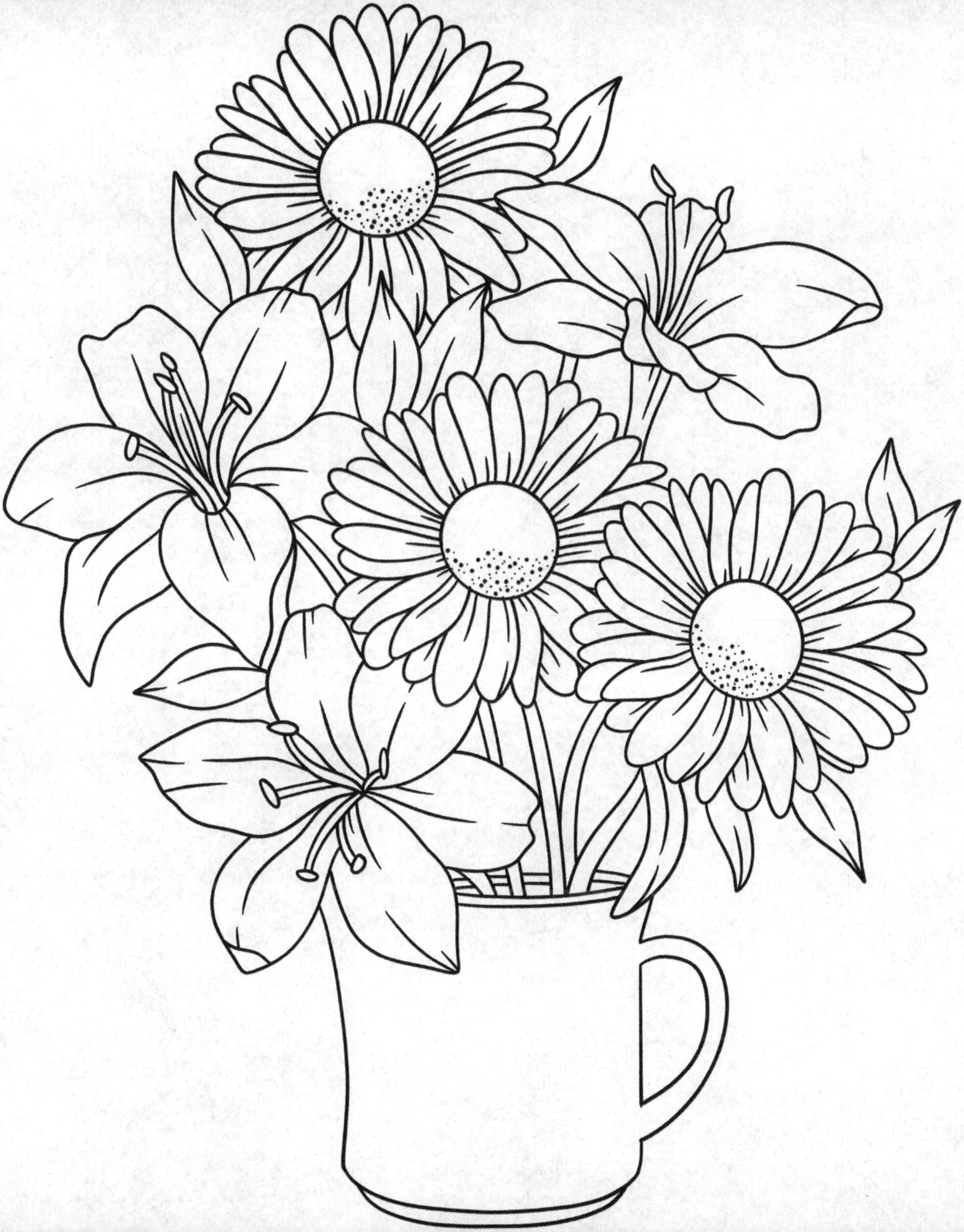

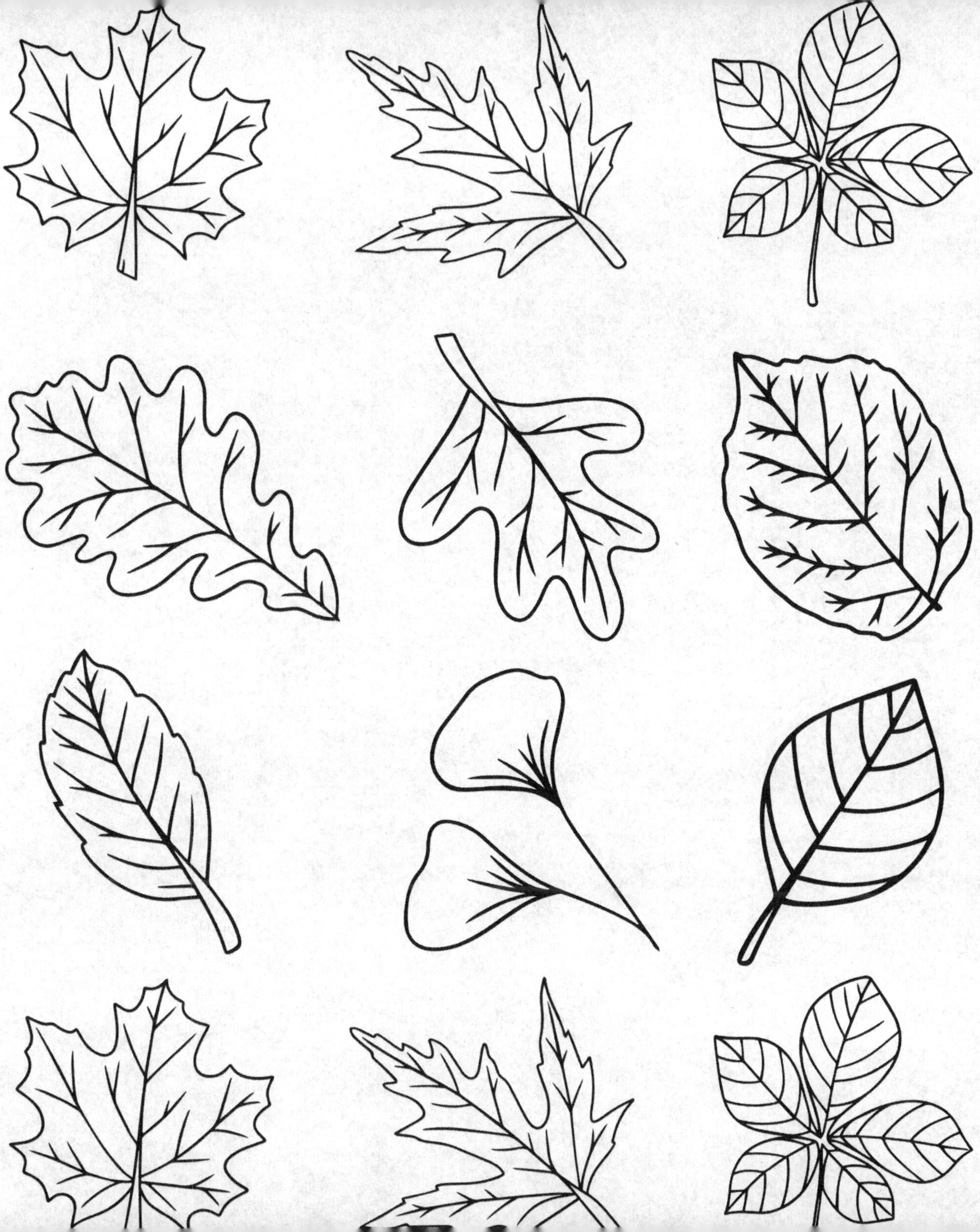

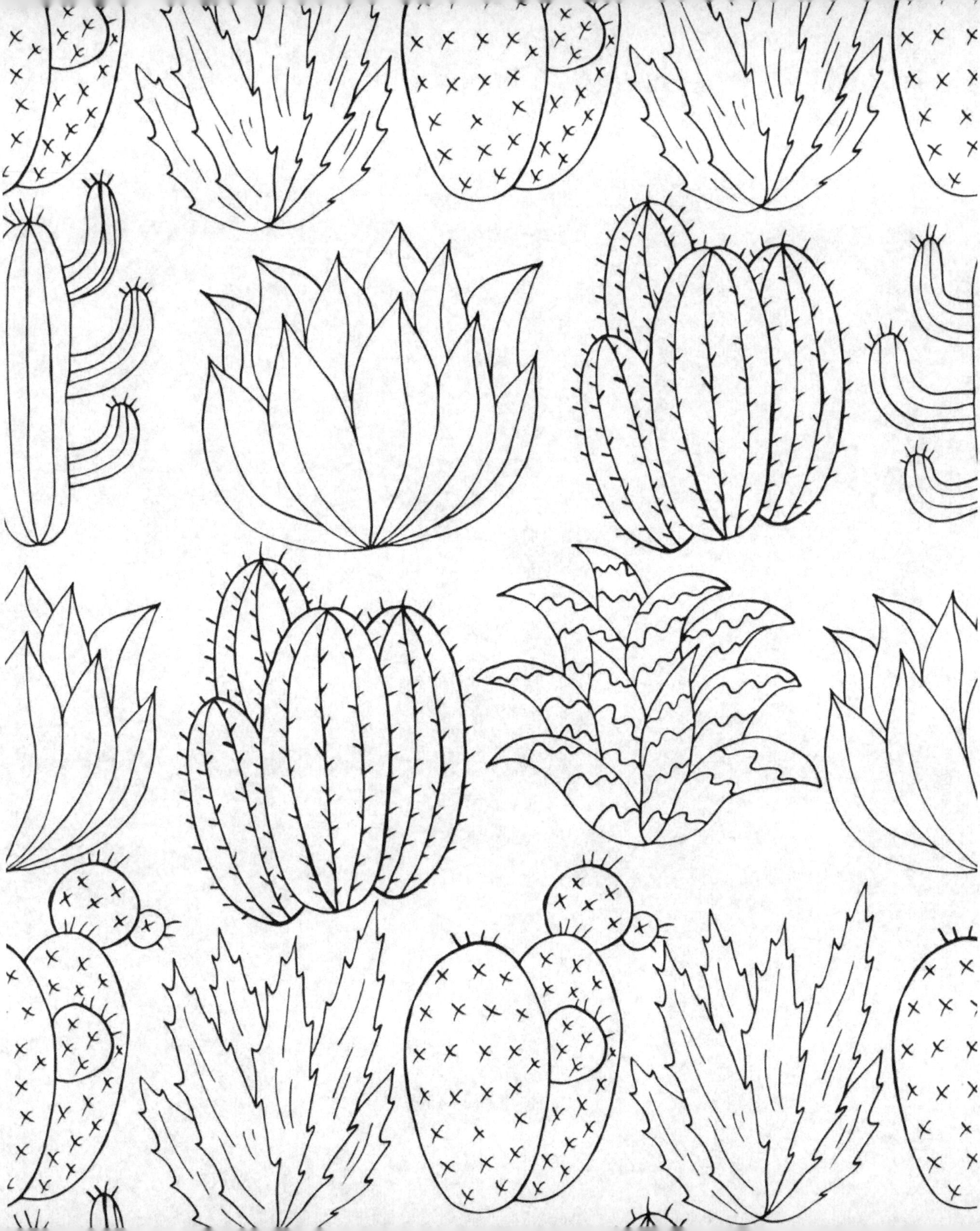

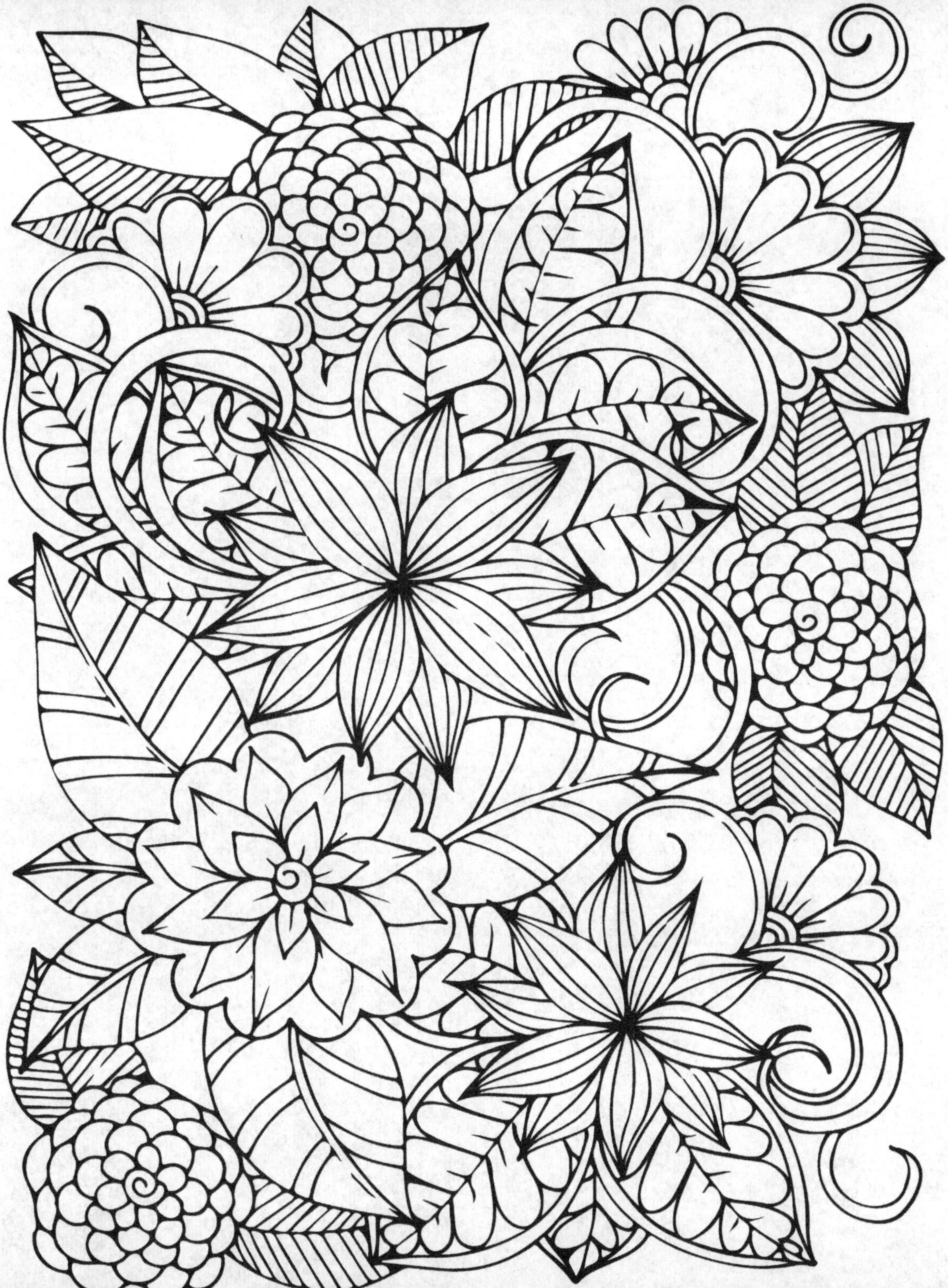

Made in the USA

Made in the USA
Las Vegas, NV
16 December 2024

14458514R00050